I'm Still Here ... Do You Hear Me?

Corinne and *Vicki* Van Meter

Copyright © 2015 by Corinne Van Meter
Cover design by Tor Lowry
All rights reserved
ISBN : 0692474501
ISBN-13: 9780692474501
Printed in the United States of America

Imagine coming to a planet from somewhere else in space and time to see what living there is like. Imagine doing something BIG early on in that worldly existence that catches the attention of the whole planet. Then, imagine disappearing into the crowd of people who live there to observe, undercover, what it feels like to be fully human. Now, imagine leaving the planet also in a BIG way, and then whispering all you learned while you were there to someone who could hear you, until she heard you so loudly she had to write a book with you, telling people how to make living in that world so much better, so much easier for everyone. Hey, it's the truth! The Earth is that planet, and this is that book. Come, let me whisper in your ear, because I'm still here ... do you hear me?

Also by Corinne Van Meter

Is it Dusk or Is it Dawn: A Hopeful Journey Through Grief

The Little Girl Who Wanted to Fly

Catapult

Also by Vicki Van Meter

Taking Flight

For
Victoria, my daughter
Betty Louise and John Paul Loboda, my parents
and
my incredible Earth family
Jim, Elizabeth and Daniel

When I live with an open heart, I am remembering and celebrating you, for you make your home in the never-ending place where all of life lives—a place called love.

ACKNOWLEDGMENTS

It was with the help of many friends that the messages in this book have been released to the world. I am indebted to my book designer Tor Lowry for the gift of his time and expertise in creating not only this book, but others—with more to come, I hope. My editor Barbara Hanks has not only given me her best on each page, but also enthusiastically supported a vision for my future even before I knew it was there. I thank Ann Cummins, my friend, whose heart has been there with mine every step of the way. To my friend and advisor Kasey Wallis, I am in deep appreciation to you for your profound insight which you so willingly share with me on this journey. I am forever thankful for my friend Reverend Elizabeth Forrest who walks the spiritual path along with me and always makes my light shine more brightly. And I am grateful for the encouragement of all the cheerleaders along the way over these past few years who have been waiting for this book to be born. And so it is . . . .

There is no place where we can go and be separate from God's care. Whether we live on one side of the veil or on the other is of no importance except to those few people who temporarily will miss our physical presence. But very soon, when that sense of absence is healed, nothing is changed, no one has lost anything... for in God, life and death are the same. To understand (that) there is no difference between life and death brings about an understanding of the meaning of immortality.

Joel S. Goldsmith, *A Parenthesis in Eternity*

TABLE OF CONTENTS

A Word From the Authors xiii

Chapter 1 Joy ………………………………………………….. 1

Chapter 2 Possibility ………………………………………….. 33

Chapter 3 Conflict …………………………………………….. 69

Chapter 4 Hiding ……………………………………………... 115

Chapter 5 Endings and Beginnings …………………………….. 153

The Little Lantern …………………………………………….. 175

A WORD FROM THE AUTHORS

Corinne

My daughter, Victoria Louise Van Meter, left this plane of existence by her own choosing on March 16, 2008. The papers say March 15, but we know it was actually the 16th, a very special day for our family. She was born into new life somewhere else, on her father's Birth on Earth Day, as I have grown to call it. In my first book, *Is it Dusk or Is it Dawn*, I conveyed our family's journey through the grief that followed Vicki's passing. I also shared the higher understanding that life, indeed, continues after we leave this earthly path. Vicki's energy continues to follow me on a daily basis; she speaks within my thoughts and enters through the words that flow from my fingers onto the keys of my computer. She has asked me to share her story to reveal the light within it.

In her earthly life, Vicki made international news as a young girl. In 1993, at age 11, she piloted a single-engine airplane across the USA. And the following year, at 12, she became the youngest female ever to pilot a single-engine airplane across the Atlantic Ocean. Now, as she continues to maneuver within the dimensions, she willingly offers to help us along our pathways while we journey on this earth 'plane' that is flying through time and space.

Last spring I sat across from my friend, Ann, at a noisy restaurant, and Vicki paid us a visit we will never forget. Her presence was measured by the tingles and bumps we felt all over our bodies, and by the words of direction that came through my voice into our hearts. Believe it or not, she laid it all out for us that evening. She outlined this book and its purpose, and she assembled it for me to see in my mind's eye. She instructed me to *plan, prepare, and get it out,* and these past two years, she has been patiently waiting for our family to be ready to complete this task. Oh, and she also asked me to include some humor in it! Now is the time for our collaboration to unfold. I am honored to assist her in this new journey of creation. I am just grateful to be in the space to be able to do so.

Vicki's first thirteen years were ones of extraordinary accomplishment, and although she continued to be ambitious and successful in her second thirteen years, many times of challenge and conflict faced her. She shares some of the truths of it all from her new, higher perspective in hopes that it will help you.

Some may think that what follows on these pages comes not from Vicki, but from my imagination, or perhaps from my higher self, but is not the source the same? Call it what you will, all truth flows from the One, the Creator, God: all wisdom, all knowledge, all understanding, all life. We are all a part of it. It does not matter what you choose to believe. I welcome you to believe whatever you desire. Search within your heart for your answers, for that is where you will find them. Allow yourself to open the door to new possibilities.

Vicki

You may have seen me once a long time ago on television, or read about me in a book at school, or maybe discovered me somewhere on the Web. I did something a few times that made the news. And maybe you read my obituary in the paper. That's when I decided to transform—leave the earth. Some say I am dead, buried, gone. You can call me what you want, believe what you want, but I tell you, I'm still here. My story is everyone's, and everyone's story is mine. I'm really just the same as you. I am you. I'm one of your friends. I just look different now. Well, you just can't see me.

Aside from the fact that my mother now hears me and wants to help me speak, I want to talk now because I'm in a position to see a lot of things differently. I can look at myself more clearly, and at you, too. I've had some time to explore it all. Actually, there is no time here. You guys live a very slow life there. It's faster here than you can imagine, and boy, do I like traveling fast! I guess with all the flying, I was prepared for it., Or was I prepared to fly there, because I came from here*? Hmmm. Well, you can figure that one out, or not! I can't tell you everything, but then again, if I did, you wouldn't believe me anyway. I guess I could just fly around here and live in bliss. We all could—here on this side of things— but we don't because you all matter to us. What happens to you, matters to the whole of All-That-Is. I know that sounds, well, off-the-wall to some, but believe me, what lies beyond the playground you are on there is so vast. There is no way to explain it. Just know that it is, and one day you will see ... if you choose to see.*

You may believe that I left before my time, but, like I said ... there is no time, and hold on ... there is no space, either! Yep, it doesn't exist here in the real world, the one you can't see. You live in a slow, solid place, enjoyable for the moment in never-ending time that we all live in when we're there, but I digress.

Back to my decision to leave: It really was my decision to make. I guess somehow I knew I could do more from where I am now. After all, you are reading this, and you probably never would have given me a second thought had I not left. I would have faded away in an old memory, perhaps.

I'll be sharing some things in the italicized parts of this book that you might not want to hear, or there is the possibility that you might not get what I'm saying. I'll be doing some soul speaking. You might find it all hard to believe, and that's your choice. You always have the freedom of choice. That's a big one; it was for me when I was there, where you are now. I offer that choice to you now along with some new perspectives. Hey, a kid flying an airplane seemed impossible when I did it. Maybe there are lots of things that seem impossible there, but in the real reality they are quite natural. The important thing about my life isn't what I did, but who I am, and the same goes for you, too.

There are pluses and minuses in everyone's life. I decided to make both of mine pretty darned big, and I got them out of the way pretty fast, too. The trouble is, you can't see which is the plus and which is the minus, can you? From where you are, it's hard to see that it's all good. The neat part of the trip for me now is that because you are reading this I get to turn what you see as the minuses into the pluses right before your eyes! I'm gonna try to help you see and help you hear, but it's really up to you. And let's lighten up and not be so darned serious, either! You know, pigs really do fly ... we'll explain that later.

Corinne

We are both grateful you have found this book. We offer it to you as a gift, one that we hope will help you to see the happenings in your life with new vision and deeper meaning. We have an important suggestion for you before you begin, however. We ask that you read without judgment or comparison of 'right' or 'wrong'. We also welcome you to read it more than once to fully tap into its hidden messages. May your understanding bring to you only life's highest and best.

Love and Light,

Corinne and **Vicki**

Joy

Joy is that place you go inside your heart

where the thing that gives you life

is resting like a soft summer day

just waiting for you to come inside and play in it.

The Little Lantern

There was a little lantern lit by the sun,
Its brilliance shone far and wide, but its work
    wasn't done.
This special little lantern made a journey to earth
And shined its light so very bright from the moment of
    its birth.

It came with a message from its Creator above.
It was filled with all possibility wrapped in a blanket of
    love.
Light disguised in a little lantern, now, who would have
    thought
Oh, the importance of that message, the one the little
    lantern brought.

I think I'll shake this family up . . .
I think I'll rock the world . . .
Somehow, I'll make it happen!
Bang!
And so it is . . .

On the day that Victoria Louise Van Meter was born, it seems to me that all the Earth chuckled, and the man in the moon grinned even wider in a 'just you wait and see' kind of smile. How perfect. Perfect. I remember being at the end of my labor when a horrendous ice storm waved its hand over our part of the nation. In the western Pennsylvania town where we lived, there was always rain, clouds and snow for a great part of the year, but this was March, and I had so hoped that the spring with its daffodils and crocuses would come soon for my new little one and the rest of the family. We were iced in, I was overdue and my husband Jim's back had gone out carrying a bed down from the attic of the third floor of our home for my mother, my fount of wisdom. What a master, my mother. I was looking forward to **her** arrival, too.

After days of carefully climbing over ice with bags of groceries, Jim finally recovered, and all was in place for baby's entrance into the world. My mother was there, and seven-year-old Elizabeth and three-and-a-half-year-old Daniel were prepared for a new brother or sister. Back then, you didn't know which one you were getting. At ten days past my due date I was ready, indeed! And, it was my birthday. Would the little one, who I suspected was a boy, arrive on my birthday or three days later on Jim's birthday? Babies come when they want to, for the most part. After all the delays, all the waiting, I remember being a bit angry as I marched militantly along the main street of our town trying to make it happen in those evening hours of my birthday. It didn't have to happen on that day, it just had to happen … and of course, eventually it did.

Surprise world—I'm a girl! And I was born on your birthday after all, Mom, at almost the same time, in the hour before midnight. Let the games begin! This game isn't like one of those wheels in Las Vegas where it spins around and lands at a random place; the wheel knows where it's going to land. I knew what I was doing; the family just didn't know yet.

We were a family whose focus was on our children, and Jim and I both wanted it that way. Although I held a teaching degree, I was an active stay-at-home mom for about 24 years. I felt that my mission was to assist my children on their chosen paths, and I enjoyed all the directions into which they led me. I guess I knew that somewhere down the line I would be using my talents in other ways. I didn't exactly know how, but that was okay. I trusted that all would be revealed in time.

At the time I grew up, most mothers stayed at home and tended to the children. My mother certainly did. She was our nurturer, listener and communicator. She shared her wisdom with us way past the time my father left the earth, which at 56, was much too early. She carried on through the many trials in her life with a strength that I aspire to match. Back then, only fathers worked, and their contribution was to support the family financially. They were respected, honored and loved for it. That's the way it was in my family. My parents created a loving environment in which to raise my two brothers, two sisters and me, as evidenced by the successful and happy grown-up lives each of us have, along with our spouses, 15 grandchildren, plus 12 great-grandchildren so far.

Jim was a real worker for our family, supporting all our pursuits to the best of his ability. He enabled us to have exciting and enriching experiences, both separately and together. His zest for life encouraged all of us to welcome adventure into our lives.

My husband's family was a bit different than mine. Although his father spent his time working, his mother also worked outside the home. That was certainly not the norm, especially then, as Jim is ten years older than I am. He was used to seeing a woman do some things 'outside the box'. His mother was the one who taught him woodworking skills, and to this day he still greatly admires her for that. He also saw the prejudice that she experienced in the workplace, and when he later became a supervisor in a large chain of restaurants he favored hiring and rewarding women in many leadership roles because he understood these things. He was and is a strong supporter of women, and his daughters have benefited from it.

And so it was that we merged our two styles of family, as all families do. I was the water, the calming influence, Jim the fire, and it seemed that Vicki found in it a blend of sensitivity and strength—deep understanding and no fear.

You see, this energy that is you goes down there, squeezes into a little body, and then it has a lot of learning to go through and teaching to do. Oh, and it decides where it will do the learning and the teaching and also chooses the people around it. So, go figure, you aren't in your family by accident; you picked them. Yes, you did, so give them a break, and yourself, too. I needed a mix of talent, personality, fearlessness and humor to pull this off, and figured you were the ones. After all, we all agreed to it beforehand when we were all here.

Vicki was born with a sense of humor, a great one. Some people are just like that. They bring joy to those around them; they just make people smile. Vicki had that magic. She may have also inherited a bit of silliness from her father. He was always accused of ruining all family pictures with crazy faces. Come to think of it, there is definitely a similarity there. We went wild over family pictures, having regular portraits done of each of the three children as they grew. Elizabeth, our first, a perfect subject, always posed appropriately, smiling when instructed to do so. She could follow direction. Daniel's approach was quite different. He took life even more seriously, and eliciting a smile from him while posing for a picture was almost impossible. It just didn't make sense to him. As a result, he cooperated for the first picture only, and all the other poses resulted in a sullen, quizzical face that said, "Why are you doing this?" And then there was Vicki—a different animal altogether. Our family photographer felt her magic as he posed our little pixie with her sleekly coifed bob, grinning her devilishly alluring smile at him through the lens as he expected an award-winning picture from this perfect moment. But then it would happen: Just as he snapped the camera, her tongue would stick out and curl around her upper lip, or she would purse both her lips, or move a hand, ruining what was supposed to be the money shot! It happened every time! It was like she was saying with a hidden smile, "Ahh, the best laid plans—foiled, once again!" We got used to purchasing some odd picture selections, but that was Vicki, and we sure did love her spirit; everyone did. There is one particularly memorable picture of her, taken one Christmas when she was three. It was taken at our Victorian home that was all dressed up for the holidays: freshly cut tree trimmed with our favorite ornaments and the colored balls shining under the lights circling the pine boughs. Vicki had a photo taken in front of the tree wearing a long red flannel nightgown with a matching red ruffled nightcap trimmed in white lace. She is leaning forward, looking right into the camera with a sparkle in her eyes and mischief behind her smile. It's a classic. It's Vicki. She was born to push some envelopes. That's Vicki.

You better believe it, people. I didn't come there to sit around. I came there to enjoy life. You did, too, all of it, every part! And my parents, they loved me, that's for sure. Sometimes I thought a little too much. I had to teach them some things.

When Vicki was just two, Elizabeth had some fun with her. Elizabeth, always the dramatist, and having quite a stockpile of creativity to offer the world, made it her mission to convince Vicki that she, Vicki, was a pig. The family got a kick out of it because it did appear that Vicki believed it. I remember taking her to the YMCA for swimming lessons when she was about three, and as the little ones lined up in the water near the edge of the pool, the lady instructor glided along beside them, asking each child's name, spending a bit of time getting acquainted and building trust. "And what's your name, sweetheart?" I heard her gently ask my daughter. Vicki unabashedly replied, "I'm Vicki-toria-the Pig!" "What?" the woman quizzed back. With no hesitation and no doubt in her voice, Vicki answered back, "I'm Vicki-toria the Pig!!" So the teacher moved on, and I can't, now, remember what she ended up calling our little 'swine', but Vicki's imagination did allow her to believe that she was a pig for quite a while.

Vicki's insistence on being a pig served as a source of amusement to the family. She assumed that role until Jim took her to the county fair to see the world's largest pig. It was huge, and coarse hair covered its enormous body. I believe it was then that she dropped the name and the image, but, as Vicki had quite a sense of humor, she was lovingly and aptly nicknamed "Hammy" by her family and friends, and she responded positively to that name as she grew older. Her pig memorabilia collection grew as the years continued to pass by.

Sense of humor! Duh. Don't you get it? How do you know I wasn't laughing at you? Maybe I knew then I would be flying. You know, pigs really do fly. Use your imagination! Well, I guess you really do. From here, I can see you imagining lots of things for yourself—things like illness and lack and hate and fear. But you know, you can use your imagination to create all the good stuff,

too.

Being in Vicki's presence was a natural set-up for fun. She just had that way about her—she was so unpretentious and had this little-kid 'cool' about her—in the way she looked, in her choice of dress, and in the manner in which she behaved. You just had to be prepared to loosen up and have some fun around her because she was a character, one who found humor everywhere. You laughed with her, and when she smiled, her eyes would twinkle, and the world would shine more brightly. Her way of finding humor in all situations followed her throughout her life, and I dare say that many along her journey would attest to it. A belly laugh with Vicki was, well, like joy released from the soul—an experience of deep connection. The seriousness with which she had fun was always an important part of her life.

A Pee-Wee Herman craze struck the nation in the '80s. Our family loved watching his movies. We even had a ventriloquist doll of our beloved Pee-Wee. Elizabeth could adeptly perform the entire script of the film, *Pee-Wee's Big Adventure,* imitating him to a tee, and Vicki, as a precocious four-year old, then began imitating her older sister's imitations of Pee-Wee. Well, one lovely Easter morning when my brothers and sisters, along with their children, gathered at my mother's house in Ohio, Vicki outdid herself. My brother-in-law, along with his video camera, was filming the youngest of the clan wearing their Easter finery, sitting outside on the porch swing before we left for Easter Sunday church services. Nobody knew what humor lay in this gem of film production until it was later viewed by all on the living room television. It's one of those *America's Funniest Home Videos* moments. Vicki in her pretty little Easter dress, black patent leather shoes, and a brimmed, straw hat, performing Pee-Wee to perfection for the camera, using her own script. Every time we see it, we all erupt into non-stop laughter. I realize all little four-year- olds do cute things, but Vicki could pull something special out of the sky! Maybe we will send that video in to AFV sometime.

Let's keep them laughing, even now. You guys still crack up when you look at that, and so do I! I can feel your laughter, you know—your happiness—your joy. I live there. I'm so glad I did that then so it can bring you joy now.

Now, this is a little family secret that I am going to share: Before Vicki could manage going into a public restroom on her own, we developed a little cooperative family system. If I took her into the women's restroom, I had to prepare the seat with paper, and then I'd lift her up onto the seat, making sure everything was sanitary. It was an involved process, and sometimes we were in a hurry. Sometimes she was in a hurry. Sometimes I was in a hurry. Anyway, the solution was this: Jim would take her into the men's restroom, lift her up so she wouldn't make contact with the seat, and then proceed to hold her until what needed to be done was finished. It would all happen with far more ease than my method over in the ladies' room. Vicki had a short haircut, and she used to wear a baseball cap, so it was decided that for those occasions, in order to conform to her surroundings, she would use the alias name of Dave. This system worked well until it was obvious that she could handle everything by herself. But none of us ever forgot Vicki's code name: Dave.

Yes, you remember it, too. I have fun playing with this little fact later on in the book....

Vicki loved animals. She even became a vegetarian early in her life because of it. We were a family of animal lovers. The procession of Van Meter animals began with a guinea pig named Ewok who lived for a short time in the children's playroom until our first rabbit, who lived in a neighboring cage, started making clandestine midnight jumps to visit Ewok. The pig went a bit crazy, and we were forced to find a nice home for him with our babysitter.

Later, we were shocked, along with the babysitter, to find out that Ewok was a girl and that she was pregnant! Never figured out how that happened! Vicki loved Ewok, but she did use his inability to speak to her advantage when 'someone' scribbled in crayon on the wall in the hall outside the playroom. Neither Elizabeth nor Daniel had ever done anything of that nature when they were small, and both were way past any thoughts of doing such a thing. So it was pretty obvious who did the deed, but when Vicki was confronted with the question, she informed us that "Ewok did it." Upon further questioning, her statement changed to, "Ewok *made* me do it." Perhaps Ewok flipped out over those nightly rabbit visits, I don't know. Maybe Vicki had some kind of communication with Ewok and he really did force her into committing the unthinkable, but at least she told the truth in the end, no matter the detours along the way. I do know that she had a great imagination.

Then there was Goldie, the goldfish that wouldn't die, no matter how dirty its water got before I changed it; Bryce, another rabbit, who succumbed to heatstroke because we weren't smart enough to know better; Toby, the gerbil, who caught a cold and left us after Vicki proudly took him to school for a pet show; Sammie, the bird, whose heart was broken when we foolishly got another bird to keep him company; a procession of mice; and Hermie, the—you guessed it—hermit crab. I think we all remember the day after school when Vicki rushed home with a friend to introduce her to Hermie. She raced up to her room and then ran downstairs to tell us that Hermie was out of his shell and he wasn't moving. That was a bit of a trauma. Eventually, for Christmas one year, the children got Cricket, a miniature Schnauzer, who was a loyal companion to us, and Elizabeth received Lucy, a cat, from Grammie. Lucy hung in there with us for 17 years. And then there was Amelia—a later addition—a cat who left us at age 18.

And how can I forget all the stuffed animals Vicki collected and loved so very much—each one so important to her. There was a time when, every night, she would tuck one special animal into bed on Jim's and my pillows. We would see them when the children were fast asleep and it was our turn to end our day. It was so loving of her—like she was taking care of us. Vicki went on in her life to have many other 'real' animals. It seemed as though they were essential parts of her life.

Look, our pets are taking care of us. They are little messengers in our lives to remind us that we are loved, and they give us the opportunity to give love unconditionally. A win-win. And about those stuffed ones—what's real, anyway? It's love, people; the rest disappears. It's only an illusion—like a giant magic trick.

We parents can be so busy being parents that we can forget or not notice that some of our greatest teachers are surrounding us—our children. We are also students learning about life, and it is only wise for us to remember *that* even if we are in these big, grown-up bodies! As the years have passed, I clearly recognize that each of my children, in his or her own way, has been a teacher for me. In Vicki's case, instruction began early on. Maybe it was because she was my youngest child, but perhaps there is more to it than that. I am just grateful I took the time to notice one of the greatest lessons I received from her very early on in her life.

Vicki was just four or five when we went shopping to purchase a new pair of blue jeans for her. The two of us started perusing the racks for styles to take into the dressing room. Vicki was, and continued to be in her life, a no-frills type of person. Hands down, she preferred straight, plain blue jeans. But I thought that Vicki, with her lean frame, would look just perfect in a lacy, embellished, feminine style that was popular at the time. So I encouraged her to at least try on a pair, just to see if she might like them.

We both took our choices into the dressing room, and when she slipped her favorite pair onto her little body, there was not only a smile on her face, but a sense of satisfaction that was apparent in the way she looked at herself in the mirror. I hated to interrupt her bliss, but I encouraged her to give my selection a try. As she secured the frilly travesty in place on her figure I could see that the joy on her face vanished, even though she didn't make any fuss about it. I, the adult in this power struggle, attempted to influence her by complimenting my choice profusely and becoming excited over her appearance. Then, I coyly posed THE question, "Which ones should we buy?" Vicki had no problem answering, "The first ones," foiling my attempts to control her mind.

Looking back on it, I know that I pouted in my response, trying to manipulate her into changing her mind when I retorted, "Maybe we should come back another time." She saw through me. She knew what I was getting at, and my four-year-old child calmly called me on it, wisely asking *me* a question instead: "Mother, whose choice is it?" I never forgot that. Indeed, whose choice is it?

So, parents, listen to what your little ones say; they can teach you a lot. They aren't totally messed up yet. And watch what you say to them, and what you think, 'cause they are so perceptive, they'll pick it all up and stuff it deep into their minds just like ... a little piggy filling his little belly eatin' slops.

When Vicki was probably five, she used to accompany Jim to our farm. Well, we called it 'the farm'. We owned some property out in the country about 20 minutes away from our current home. Jim and I had spent our early married life there, first living in a mobile home, and later building a beautiful brick home next to a lake that Jim incorporated into a campground business he had started years before. After that business ended, he got a job as a salesman in a small town nearby where we ended up living for the next 33 years. Ever the entrepreneur, at the same time he held his sales job, he started a restaurant in a building right next to where he worked. I was stuck out in the country with a baby, Elizabeth, and it became clear that we needed to be closer to civilization, so we moved into town, but maintained ownership of some of the property in the country. Jim liked to relax by working on the land. He planted thousands of Christmas trees, cleared paths, mowed fields—he enjoyed it all for some time until we finally sold everything.

It was a special time for Jim and little Vicki on a Saturday, perhaps, that they hopped into the family van and made the trek to 'the farm' to be together in the natural world. She wore her coonskin cap, carried a hatchet, pretended to smoke—which neither of us did—and experienced a bit of the outdoors with her dad. Then, on Sundays, she sat in church with the family in 'our row' right in front of the pulpit, and while the minister gave his sermon she quietly drew pictures of Army men, tanks and guns on the church bulletin. The family behind us saw it all. There was no doubt: Vicki was a wild card.

I was the last one in the bunch, and I came to support these people, you know. It may not have seemed that way, but it was my deal to come there and shake them all up. And looking at it from here, I certainly did.

Vicki adored her big sister and big brother, and the feeling was mutual. She so looked up to Elizabeth, who was seven years older. Elizabeth was accomplished in school, in sports, in all the activities she attempted, and Vicki both admired that in her and perhaps, patterned her own goal-setting after the example of her sister. Elizabeth was a fine first child to lead her younger siblings forward in their journeys. Of course, there comes a time in everyone's life when they must branch off into their own thinking, making their own choices, and that is as it should be. And Daniel, only three years older than Vicki, was her buddy. She even shared a room with him for a time, sleeping in a trundle bed next to his, surrounded, interestingly, with red, white and blue wallpaper embellished with all types of airplanes. As a child, she followed Daniel around, playing with the guys, collecting comic books and Star Wars figures, all of them having a grand time using their imaginations. She and Daniel also shared a deep love of animals.

The morning of Vicki's kindergarten pictures I fixed her now pixie haircut to match the tiny, mischievous, but sweet child that she was. She insisted that I spike her hair like her brother's. I mean, insisted! Remembering her lesson to me on choice, I did just that, and I felt a bit off my rocker when I delivered her to her classroom that morning. Vicki could pull off any kind of a look; she just had that way about her. She looked cool in odd combinations, but this was picture day! What kind of a mother would let her daughter spike up her hair for a picture that would live on as a kindergarten memory? Me, mother of Vicki Van Meter, that's who. When the pictures came back, we all decided on retakes, even Vicki, but we still have that one picture in which she looked just as she had wanted to look that morning. I love looking at that picture…it makes me smile.

As I said, Vicki always brought out the fun wherever she went and had a way of drawing everyone close. She was tough, determined, and tenacious with her sister and brother. There was a game the children played anytime we traveled on a vacation or to visit my mother and the other aunts, uncles, and cousins staying at Grammie's house on holidays. The game: Rock-Fighter, their response to the popular *Rocky* movie. The stage was set like this: the seats in the back of the van were made flat so the kids could lie down on blankets and pillows. Nowadays, everyone must be belted in, and that's a good thing, but our children really enjoyed those relaxed laws and the freedom it brought them to play. Let the games begin! One would take on another. It had to be Elizabeth against one or both of them, as she was the oldest, and sometimes it was tag team between Daniel and Vicki. Jim and I didn't watch; he couldn't, and I certainly didn't want to see this spectacle, but we heard it all, and it proceeded until I would eventually call it off. The thing is, these competitions got pretty ferocious. I mean, it was serious stuff, and Vicki—little Vicki—would inevitably end up in the well near the door, but somehow she would always manage to come back into the ring, and she never whined or complained. They gave her a run for her money, but then again, she did the same for them, too.

Which came first, the chicken or the egg? Yep, games are fun. I'll tell you what the real game is: your chance to be there in that life. It is a game—a game of opportunity to experience all kinds of feelings, and it's fun, too! Hey, it's why you are there.

Funny how you can remember obscure moments from decades ago. I recall riding in a big yellow school bus on the way to Foxcroft Elementary School. Pictures of the route are emblazoned on my mind. I can see one stop with a miniature cabin playhouse in the backyard; waves of memory fill me and I am once again inside, imagining, pretending in all the wonder and possibility on the other side of that tiny door, just the same as I had done each day on my bus ride! Just the thought of it still delights me. I remember I often made my own special sanctuary on the sloping yard outside the back door of our house. I'd lean an umbrella on its side, then add some boxes underneath for furniture. If it rained it was especially cozy inside with my body curled in a ball, keeping warm as the water splattered on my rooftop and poured around me making its way down the hill. I felt safe enjoying the refreshment of the rain, feeling the sensations it brought. My house was intact, and I was content despite the absence of the warmth of the sun. On sunny days my sister, brother and I, along with some neighborhood kids, might make a house in the center of the clump of trees in the empty field that lay across the street or somewhere on the moss secluded in the nearby woods. Making houses. Imagining. Pretending. Are the children telling us something? Maybe we should be enjoying playing our games inside the houses we create, no matter where the house or what the game.

Very good, Mother. See, you remember things like that for a reason. They mean something if you look at them, pay attention, and see the lesson.

Our family was one big Disney-loving machine! My husband and I discovered Walt Disney World in Florida with Elizabeth when she was two, and we all fell deeply and hopelessly in love. Of course, as our family grew we returned to our favorite place on the planet more times than I can even now remember, and consequently we knew it all by heart, every nook and cranny. It was much smaller back then, and through the years we learned how to use our time wisely and make the most of our trips. We prided ourselves in being Disney World experts! When Vicki was just old enough to make the trek along with the family, she had to endure us older ones whipping her around all the parks at top speed in our 'wisdom', but on that first trip, she still managed to catch all the magic of the moments. Back then, it was either the Magic Kingdom or Epcot Center, and Vicki's favorite seemed to be Epcot. Even as a youngster she had an expanded way of thinking, I guess. Although she adored all the characters roaming the grounds, she was particularly taken with the offerings at all the various countries at Epcot. Perhaps something inside of her knew she would be visiting many of them as she got a little older. Her biggest fascination by far at Epcot was the imagination pavilion. She loved the character, Figment. We have a picture of her with the magician-like man who sometimes stood outside the building and entertained the exiting crowds with a puppet of Figment, while plops of water jumped in a water feature nearby. We bought a stuffed Figment for Vicki, and he remained a special treasure to her throughout her life. I can remember sewing up his long neck a number of times, returning him to a survivable state. Figment was a figment of imagination, and Vicki certainly had one!

That being said, although Vicki had been there a few times already by the time she was in second grade, she hadn't had the total immersion yet, so we took a trip to paradise together—just Vicki and me. We stayed on the grounds at the Polynesian Hotel where we had the chance to ride boats, swim, play on the beach, enjoy a luau, and for the first time Vicki had a leisure experience at the Magic Kingdom and Epcot Center. She was drawn to the giant globe, the world that is the center of Epcot, and she delighted in every wonderful discovery she made in this playground. Now there was time to take in all the characters dressed in the costumes of different countries, and of course, her face beamed at seeing her favorite, Figment, that funny little creature who bounced around on a ride where a kaleidoscope of color and ideas was the prevailing theme. A figment of the imagination. She loved him; I could feel her excitement. She soaked it all in as if it would sustain her. She couldn't get enough, it seemed, and neither could I.

That time with her was so precious to me then, and it remains a beautiful memory in my life. We were enveloped in a dream together. I can still see her standing in the darkness in front of the big fountain in Epcot with the water splashing behind her, the colored lights and space-age music surrounding us, as I took her picture and read in her being the sadness of leaving this magical place that we had together shared.

Earlier that evening she sat across from me at our dinner table in France's pavillion where we had the last meal of our trip. I can still see her holding close to her heart some kind of a little glowing ball we had purchased earlier, her little hands forming a triangle, with the ball at the center. I see her looking into my eyes with joy and wonder. I am grateful to remember that picture—a heart sketch.

It was great being there in all that possibility! That's what it is, you know—your imagination can create so many possibilities, and maybe I was knowing it! Hey, I loved that part of my life. Well I loved all of my life. I've come to know that every part of living there in the world is precious, even the not-so-good stuff. It only lasts for such a short time, I tell you, and it's an experience. After it's finished it's all okay because it was okay in the first place. After all, you really wanted the experience.

Hey, wait a minute, could life be a dream? 'Row, row, row your boat gently down the stream. Merrily, merrily, merrily, merrily, life is but a dream.' And Mom, the triangle at the heart, that's where the love center is. Maybe I was giving you some kind of signal—telling you something? Well, looks like you're figuring something out now.

I remember the time we all went to a concert at the college in our town. It was a special occasion for us because the pianist giving the solo concert was the piano teacher for both Daniel and Vicki. Elizabeth had taken lessons earlier, but from another teacher. We tried to expose our children to the arts as much as we could. I remember taking them to hear summer band concerts in the park in our Norman Rockwell-like town. The band played from a gazebo in the town center as townspeople gathered around, dotting the lawn on blankets, taking it all in while little children ran quietly through the crowd enjoying the music in their own way. Our children knew they were supposed to sit and listen, and each year I'd question them as to which instrument they would play when they were older, attempting to plant a seed. Music was a part of my life, and I wanted my children to experience its beauty as I had. Elizabeth chose the clarinet, and Daniel played the trumpet for a bit. Vicki had a stint on the violin, and she was quite good at it, but eventually gave it up. All of them started out on the piano. We had been fortunate that one of the members of our church was an accomplished pianist who had gone to a conservatory and was well-known for her musical ability. She was back in town giving some private lessons while she fulfilled her duties as the county beauty queen. So it was that both Vicki and Daniel began lessons with her.

The concert in question was held in an intimate setting in the lobby of one of the buildings on the campus of Allegheny College, and our highly skilled piano teacher/beauty queen was to share some of her own compositions. We prepared the children by reminding them of their teacher's accomplishments and training at a highly prestigious music school, emphasizing that it was a privilege for them to have someone of her caliber as their teacher, and it was certainly a wonderful opportunity to hear her play in this special concert. There we were with the family, sitting attentively right in front, of course, so the children could observe her closely and appreciate the measure of her talents. In dazzling dress, she impressively took her place on the bench in front of the large, black grand piano before us, and as her fingers reached out, moving over the ivory keys, we too were surprised to hear the combination of sounds that filled the air. But no soothing strains came from the keys to impress our children's waiting little ears. Instead came the sounds of dissonance, music that didn't make any sense at any level, even to us parents—sort of like one of those poems you read over and over, but you just don't get it. And equally shocking, as well as embarrassing, was to hear our two children start their own kind of symphony: laughter that went on and on and on. You know the kind of uncontrollable bubbling inside that can't be stopped, no matter what? Well, that's what happened. I can't say they didn't try to keep a lid on it; they knew better, but the chuckling did manage to escape at various times throughout the entire concert, creating a kind of music of its own. They obviously didn't have appreciation for the cacophonous sounds traveling from the piano to their ears. Probably the worst part of it was that they made us laugh, too, at them! All I can say is that it was, indeed, one of those memorable moments in our family history. Their piano lessons didn't go on for much longer. Even when they got to be grown, Vicki and her brother used to laugh together about some of the oddest things, and we didn't always get it, but they obviously did.

Yes! It was hysterical. Daniel and I went wild inside. To our parents we looked like misbehaving kids, but we both knew how hilarious it all was! Everybody's all serious, sitting there expecting this fabulous music from this brilliant musician, and here she's plunking on the keys, making crazy, off-the-wall sounds, sort of like we did when we were fooling around, and she's supposed to be so good! It sounded like a bunch of mistakes to us, and it was darned funny! What a symbol that was for seeing the absurdity in the game of life. Hey, just enjoy the whole thing, no matter how it sounds! Maybe it's supposed to be fun to screw up. Maybe a mistake is just that—a Miss Take: a perk of living in a human body. Cut! Take two, take three, take however many you want to take!

I was also a Brownie leader, as my mother was before me. Those days of camping, crafting, and learning how to do everything from babysitting to cooking to making a bed were fun times filled with positive experiences, and I wanted to carry on the tradition with my own girls. I had been a leader for Elizabeth, a helper for Daniel in the Cub Scouts, and I was a co-leader for Vicki's troop for a couple of years. One year I directed the children in a small play that was to be performed for the parents of our little Brownie Girl Scouts. Based on Vicki being, well, Vicki, everyone knew she deserved to have the leading role in the production. The girls were supposed to memorize their lines. Most of them had shorter lines to learn, but Vicki had a ton of them, and she readily absorbed each one. Actually, it was quite amazing how natural it all was for her.

At group practice, everything ran smoothly with no problems. Then came the afternoon of the big performance, and the girls were well into the play when someone made a critical mistake that had the potential to throw Vicki off and sidetrack the whole play. Well, it was something to see her stand before a group and calmly remain in character and totally ad-lib her way through the crisis until all of them got on the right track once again. Her quick mind and ease of being was obvious not only to me, but to the audience, as well as the cast. It was as if she stood and held the space for everyone until they understood that it was all okay. It is a noteworthy remembrance.

Hey, do you think I was practicing for some bigger productions in my future? I'm glad you are having such a good memory, Mother. It helps explain a lot, doesn't it? Holding space ... hmm ... interesting observation ....

Vicki was in other theatrical productions when she was even younger. She was a little angel in *The Best Christmas Pageant Ever*, a show in which both Elizabeth and I had a part. She didn't say anything, she just appeared and looked cute. She also played a hopping bunny in *The Velveteen Rabbit*, and her cuteness continued to show itself. And who could forget the church Christmas pageant where she became a face-mugging shepherd? We have the picture to prove that one! I was involved in our local community theater, and it afforded some opportunities to all our children. Vicki was the captain in *James and the Giant Peach,* and I remember that in the one or two lines she had, she was captivatingly funny! She also played a paperboy in *Our Town*, sporting a period cap on her head, masking her true gender. She was used to disguising herself! Vicki eventually attended a theater camp for a couple of summers as her sister had done in previous years. The first summer, I believe she played a pirate. I can see her wearing a bandana around her head and this white and blue horizontally striped long shirt skimming her lanky, emaciated looking body, demonstrating to me just how much she missed my home cooking! The second summer she hammed it up as a mouse in a challenging speaking role. Vicki was a chameleon; she could support, but she could definitely lead, as well.

All remain great moments in Van Meter history.

Hey, like I said—life's like a big play anyway. Why not pretend in the pretend?

There was always something about Vicki that was mysterious or unknown, if you will, something hidden going on inside of her. Of course, that is as it should be. We each occupy a private place inside ourselves where no one can go. How can we truly know what someone else thinks or feels or why they do or say something? I know that Vicki had some interesting comments for us, starting from a very young age. When she was quite small, she remarked to me, "Do you remember when I was the mother and you were the child?" If I knew what I know now, I certainly would have explored that comment more. Sometimes she would talk in her sleep and seemed to be in a different world until I managed to bring her back to this one.

When she was about six, she casually mentioned to both Jim and me, "You know, I'm not going to live long." Of course, we cast that comment aside. As she continued to grow, her father would sometimes want to share something that was on his mind, and in her impatience she would retort, "I know what you are going to say!" Of course, he didn't believe her, and would then require her to tell him exactly what it was that he was thinking, and sure enough, she was right!

I just had this feeling that she was tuned into another world, that she knew much more than she was communicating to us. When she began painting at a later age, her work conveyed a great depth of feeling. She loved expressing with color, and I can see reflections of the seasons of Vicki's life in the pieces she has left behind. At the time she created them, I wasn't sure what it all meant. When you are living in life and not totally aware, well, some things pass you by—until you get it.

Hey, that's an understatement! Lots of things pass you by! I knew why I was there to begin with. I tried to get some points across to everyone—like to my mother—and prepare them, teach them. I let it slip out, but eventually I forgot, or maybe not. I just didn't say it anymore; I just knew it. Is it so hard to think that I might have known what was coming for me? Maybe I didn't talk about it because I didn't need to. Maybe I didn't get it myself, but still, could some part of me have known?

Mom, I even showed you where I was going in my paintings! Those dreams—nothing to be alarmed about! Where do you think you go in dreamtime? The real part of you has to have a break from the illusion, to reconnect! Lots of great things happen to you on the other side when you sleep. You're definitely awake there. The question for you then is, "Are you asleep when you're awake?"

All of my life I have been sensitive; I cry easily, and not because I am physically hurt. As a matter of fact, I have a high tolerance for pain. But I feel things deeply, and I suppose my reaction to it is to shed tears, and that isn't necessarily a bad thing, but I am the kind that can start the tears flowing within seconds during a commercial that touches me. Well, Vicki never liked that aspect of me. I say that, but I don't know if it's true. She seemed more to show her disapproval of it, like she expected more from me. Maybe she felt the need to show me how to conquer my feelings. When I cried in her presence I used to notice her response, and I'd end up defending myself. After all, I have a right to cry if I want to, whenever I want! I can see it differently now. She was trying to teach me to take more control over my emotions, not to avoid them, but to master them by noticing and allowing myself to lift higher and ride over my feelings, instead of letting them affect me so. Could she feel my emotions when I cried? Were we that connected? Was she 'reading' me, showing me how to be stronger—a lesson that this life's journey has certainly taught me? My power was always there in the core of me, and I needed to call upon it in order to achieve balance in my life. She was born knowing how to do it, and she was showing me how to be stronger. Could she have known that I would need to become even stronger in order to someday face the ultimate challenge of her decision to leave this world? Funny, but I don't seem to cry as much anymore.

Note to Mother: The answers to your questions are ... yes, yes, yes, and YES! Okay, so, you go there to experience and feel things, all kinds of things, and that's great, but the deal is, when you learn how to balance while you are living, it all gets easier. It's like riding a bike: It's fun once you learn to ride. You start out by looking at the bike, and you really want to ride it. You see other people doing it so easily, and you find out after you pick it up that it takes work to ride, but you keep on practicing because you know you can do it. You keep trying. Sometimes you fall, but you keep going until you learn to balance. And while you are learning on all those practice runs, you get help from your family—maybe your father or mother or someone else is willing to help you by holding you up until you learn. When you do learn to balance yourself on that bike, you can ride in freedom with the wind blowing your hair and a smile on your face! You never think of falling off anymore. You just get on and ride. Balance!

We're ALL connected. Your family, everyone else there, us, here. Look, we're all one big family. Families help each other, right? Help is all around you. Look for it, ask for it, and you will receive it! That should sound familiar because it's the truth, and the sooner you all get it there, well, the easier 'living' will be for you and everyone in the fam.

When Vicki was about eight years old, Elizabeth was enjoying success as a member of the high school forensics team. She was an outstanding speaker and dramatist, capturing many awards for her school. I had been on my own high school team and did well myself, so when the coach of the team retired, I found myself taking over the coaching position of the high school speech and debate team. The tournaments were held on Saturdays. We'd have to get up around 5:00 a.m., board a yellow school bus in the dark, and make the long trek to our destination where we'd spend the day in some fierce competition. Football and basketball had nothing on us! Being the coach, my job was to judge multiple rounds of competition. The judge must not only rank the competitors, but also write comments and suggestions to help each person improve. It can get a bit overwhelming, and for someone like myself who has a hard time making a decision, it can be excruciating. Comments and final tallies must be turned in quickly, and I would agonize over it all!

Just as Vicki spent some Saturdays with Jim, she did with me, as well. Many times she accompanied the team to a tournament and sat in a classroom along with me, listening to people give speeches, and then making decisions about their performances. She sat quietly observing. The competitors would leave the room, and my work as judge would then begin. I pored over my sheets of comments and tried to determine the ranking of the students, and invariably there would be times when I just couldn't decide between the placement of two of them. On those occasions I would turn to Vicki, and she advised me—my seven-year-old Vicki. Maybe she was even younger than that. She had such good sense, a fine eye and ear, and a connection with her intuition. I can remember the certainty of her responses. I really relied on her judgment calls, and you know, she was always right on! She smoothed out those rough times for me and made my job a bit easier. She was part of the entire team, and everyone appreciated her.

Hey, was this some foreshadowing of what I'd find myself doing some day? Everybody in the fam related to each other in a different way. Me, I was a combo of my parents. I needed to be all that in order to do what I had decided I was going to do before I came there. Of course, when you get there, you can't remember any of what you planned to do. You just go on your feelings, your instincts, and you look around at everything, people and nature, and you get reminders about who you are and what you are supposed to do, so you can stay on track. But, man, most of you down there just don't see it. Some of you get it, but some of you are asleep. Most of you just forget, and that's normal for living there. You just have to remind yourself that there is more to it all. I know, that's hard when you are in the game. I mean, I do know. I've been there, too.

Today it is not uncommon for girls to participate in all sorts of sporting endeavors. I remember going to high school in the '60s when the closest thing to a sport for girls was being a cheerleader, or maybe a majorette. We only participated in sports in gym classes. All manner of sport was definitely male. When Vicki was still in her first decade of life, girls had advanced a bit and were welcomed into playing soccer and T-ball or bantam-league ball. Boys could advance to baseball teams and girls to softball teams. Not surprisingly, Vicki was the first to break a barrier in our small town.

Hardball baseball was Vicki's love. She collected team cards, her favorite being the Cubs, and Mark Grace was her favorite player. Wearing a baseball hat and T-shirt was common dress for her. She also loved playing catch with her father and being part of a game when her brother, sister and neighborhood kids played in the backyard. Even though she was much younger than the others, she always played hard and took it quite seriously. She played in the bantam league, and it seemed she was born with lots of natural ability.

When she was old enough to sign up for Little League baseball she discovered, to her disappointment, that girls were not allowed to play hardball baseball; they were only allowed to be on a softball team. That did not set right with Vicki. She insisted that if she could not play hardball, she wouldn't play at all. She thought that the big softball was a bit more of a 'sissy' kind of ball, and she wanted nothing to do with it! Of course it isn't, as female softball players are pretty tough, but to Vicki, at that time, it was unchallenging, and it pushed her into doing something that no girl in town had yet done. One summer she masqueraded as a boy at a baseball camp at the college in our town, keeping up the deception until the final game, when to the surprise of everyone, she inadvertently removed her cap during a play, revealing her female gender!

My husband knew her skill level and identified with her 'fight', and on the day of sign-ups for the Boys Little League teams, he and Vicki stood in line along with all the boys and their fathers eager to begin the season. When they got to the desk they were informed that girls couldn't be on the team, but were instead invited to be a part of the softball program for girls. Jim questioned them. Vicki insisted—always pushing the envelope. As Vicki later told the story, she came to the conclusion that the higher-ups relented because, "They probably thought they would be sued or something."

So it was that Vicki started this pioneering journey by attending the try-outs for the boys' team picks. The would-be players fielded balls and caught flies in the junior high school gym. Jim came home jubilant with the news that Vicki had done a stellar job. He reported that out of a field of about 165 boys, she was one of the first round team picks! So Vicki started her baseball career. She went on to be an outstanding second baseman who garnered write-ups in the paper even when her team was not the winning one. At the season's end, her team won the championships in a game that showcased not only Vicki's baseball skills, but her ability to think at a higher level, when, at a critical juncture, she shocked the opposition and faked a throw that ultimately knocked one of the other team's best players out of play. Of course, it was not just Vicki who brought the win for the team, but she certainly always did her part to add to the taste of victory! The following year the coaches wanted her to become a pitcher, and then we stepped in to avoid dealing with the possible replacing of her teeth—she could really throw that ball, and she had no fear! This little girl had *no* fear! It wasn't long after that that we took the fateful ride to the little airport in our small town, and a whole new journey began. A pioneer she was . . .

I admit I was competitive when it came to sports, and besides, I really wanted to show everyone what girls could do and be. They rock! I decided that one before I got there, and I think I succeeded in showing it for the time I was there. Girls, guys—it's true—it's what's inside that counts. Hey, what is inside, anyway?

As I said earlier, we were Disney World lovers to the max! I recall another time when Vicki and I were there by ourselves, and we stayed at a hotel with a pond nearby where visitors could rent small paddle boats to cruise around the waterway. We rented one and took off on an excursion. She let me steer the boat, and shortly after taking the controls I was heading us in all directions, threatening to ground us, or at least get us stuck in the marshy areas surrounding the lake. We laughed, and Vicki took over, calmly instructing me to make only minor moves in order to make the boat take me where I wanted to go—once again trying to teach me something even deeper. She seemed amused at my inability to comprehend such an obvious course of action. Subtleties came naturally to her. I remember that when I enrolled her in tap lessons. I would laugh to myself at the way she kept all her movements small and controlled, when everyone else was flailing and open. Even when she was older, in her teens and twenties, she had a way of taking things slowly. I'd be rushing to get somewhere or do something, and she just never would allow herself to do that. She must have been amused many times at my struggle to overcompensate in so many ways. Perhaps I didn't trust enough.

Bingo, Mother, Bingo!

Vicki's elementary school years were filled with happiness. She enjoyed school, her friends, her sports, her activities, her family. She had a love of learning, and soaked it all in. One great year for her was first grade; it was there that her science-minded teacher nourished her connection to animals, as well as the environment, and her love and honoring of both only grew in the years that passed. In third grade she was introduced to the excitement of space when a guest speaker from NASA came to her classroom. That event critically impacted Vicki's life, for she set her sites on one day traveling in space. She also had an interest in historical figures and kept a large framed poster of John Fitzgerald Kennedy, her hero, on her bedroom wall. She would eventually join the United States Peace Corps, a program which was started by him, our country's 35th president. Her room was filled with collections of all sorts: stuffed animals, baseball cards, Stars Wars figures, comic books, anything Disney, Red Rose Tea figurines, Sylvanian Family animals, key chains, coins, memorabilia from vacations. It was all neatly stored in special boxes or spots scattered throughout her room, a room filled with excitement and joy. The love and encouragement Vicki received from her teachers during her formative years was priceless. Teachers—do they really know the impact their thoughts and actions have on a developing spirit?

Teachers come in many shapes and sizes, and are found in lots of places. That includes animals, rocks, trees, water, and regular people who you'd never suspect are teachers, even kids. You're all teachers for each other: it's a two-way street, you know. The most important thing you can do for someone, everyone you meet, each and every day, is to let them know how dang awesome they are, even if that is just a thought in your mind. As a matter of fact, tell it to yourself, too. The real YOU is AWESOME! Remember that.

I'M STILL HERE ... DO YOU HEAR ME?

Possibility

Anything, indeed, is possible.

You, know, pigs really can fly.

The little lantern listened to direction from back home
And brightly beamed its pure white light; over the world it roamed.
People gathered 'round to see what it could do,
To watch in awe and wonder, and feel inspiration, too.

The little lantern was able to do amazing things.
It bathed the dark in its loving light, transforming everything!
The little lantern held a secret that it hoped the people would know was true,
That everyone could use that light, for it was inside of them, too.

"Mrs. Van Meter, I'm sorry, but Vicki is not a candidate for the gifted program at school. Unfortunately, she fell short of the qualifying scores by a couple of points." That's what the counselor told me at our appointment when we discussed the results of Vicki's final testing to determine if she was eligible for her school's gifted program. Her fourth-grade teacher had recommended her for testing. Vicki had always done well in school, and we had not yet pursued the route of a gifted and talented program for her. One of Elizabeth's teachers had made a similar recommendation for her when she was back in her fifth-grade year, and I remember that the night before the test, she came to me and confided, "Mom, I'm not any better than my friends in the regular class, and I don't want to leave them." We canceled the test. I was proud of her for coming to that conclusion. But Vicki's situation was a bit different. She seemed itchy for other things to do, and being a former teacher at the time, I recognized that she could use some extra stimulation, so we followed through with the testing. When I received the results, I remember telling the counselor, "Vicki will be taking some flying lessons soon, and I think that endeavor will keep her occupied for now." How right I was!

Yes! I didn't want that anyway, not really. You know you people down there don't always see just how "smart" everyone is. I mean, really. Truth is, you've got access to all knowledge, all the great minds and thoughts that have ever been. You really are all of that! And nature, it's all around you—so much intelligence. The trouble is you guys think intelligence comes just from inside your own heads. Man, there's so much more going on. Let's have some appreciation down there. Use your resources, please! Where do you think great discoveries come from? First open up to believing and then ... know. Loosen up, connect, and remember. Easy for

me, you say, right? Well, could it all be easier than you think? Think ... LOL!

Okay, so here is where it started. I smile because I have heard Vicki in her early life relate this story countless times to so many who have asked the question, "How did you start flying?" She always patiently answered with the same concise story. Brief and to the point was Vicki's style, and people appreciated that about her. Well, this is my version: One Sunday, after church, our family drove out to our small local airport to see the new terminal building that was recently built. Vicki was ten at the time, and we all walked around inside and out seeing the new construction, which didn't take very long. We noticed there was a flight school that opened up in an adjoining building. When we got home, Vicki told me that her dad had signed her up for an airplane ride. Now, I was a bit apprehensive. My father had been an air traffic controller, but I was never even in an airplane until I was in college, except for the time my Girl Scout troop actually got to sit inside a parked one on an excursion to our local international airport. Jim earned his commercial pilot's license before I met him, but he never flew commercial craft, although he did at one time own his own small plane and enjoyed flying it recreationally on those rare moments that he wasn't working as a supervisor for a restaurant chain. This all happened before I knew him. He sold his plane to buy me my engagement ring and to start our married life together. Jim explained to me that he just wanted to give Vicki the opportunity to see if she liked being up in the air, as she had expressed an interest in some day becoming an astronaut. Jim also recognized Vicki's skill set, and being a pilot himself, he could see the possible link for Vicki, too. Neither of us held much hope that the instructors would actually call back and schedule a session with a ten-year-old, so I put it out of my mind, but sure enough, it happened. I did not want to stop Vicki from doing something she wanted to do. I guess I always felt like I should listen to what my children were saying and consider it all. Of course, I was not totally at ease with the whole idea, but I made the decision that I couldn't let my fear stand in the way of my daughter's choice, if those choices, indeed, were hers. She taught me that one earlier.

My husband was confident of her safety, and Vicki was firm in her choice. "Okay, it's only a short ride. I can do this," I thought. But, I couldn't show up at the airport to see her take off. Instead I opted to let Jim drive her there and I would be present to see her immediately after the plane landed. I remember standing on the terminal balcony watching the plane descend onto the tarmac. I hurried out to the runway to see her as she emerged from the cockpit of the little Cessna 150. I was determined to sense her true reaction when I first gazed upon her face. As she stepped out of the plane and walked toward me, I saw such a look of power on her face and in her being. I knew instantly that it was real. I can still recall that moment. So, it was to be.

My parents were there from the beginning, and they helped me get what I needed to experience in my life—the highs and the lows. Somehow they knew what was going on in my earth picture. Dang, I'm glad they listened to me.

I'd like to speak now of one very special man who also recognized in Vicki something extraordinary, for he stepped forward and guided her along what has proven to be a distinctive path on this earth. As Vicki shared her excitement about her airplane ride with me, Bob Baumgartner, her highly experienced instructor, shared with Jim his response to the flight with Vicki. She had immediately taken to the experience by listening to him and responding with a higher level of understanding and skill than most of the adults he had ever worked with in the past. He enthusiastically expressed his willingness to continue working with her, expanding her knowledge, nurturing her skills as far as they could go.

A private pilot ground school class was beginning soon and Vicki hungrily signed up for it. It would be held for ten weeks, one evening per week, and at the end of the session there would be a written test. Vicki attended the classes religiously. No one there was like her; they were all male adults, some business owners, others farmers in the area, even a county commissioner. Everyone accepted her and made her feel welcome. Vicki took her schoolwork along with her to complete when the others broke for cigarettes or to eat doughnuts. But she soon encountered her first serious hurdle: She did not pass the final test. It had been wintertime during the first round of classes, and now spring was approaching. Because she would be spending some time up in the air taking actual lessons now that the weather was improved, she made a decision to take the classes all over again. Perhaps, with the addition of actually flying, things might be easier to understand. The only catch for her was that she had to forgo participating in the upcoming basketball season at school because the schedule of games would interfere with her ground school classes. So she sacrificed something she enjoyed, but it all paid off for her when she passed the final test this time, and with a high score, I might add! Vicki had 60 hours of ground school behind her, and she definitely proved that she was self-motivated.

Choices—they matter. How you spend your 'time' there does matter. Wow, the choices you have are endless, aren't they? I did say to lots of people while I was there, "If you put your mind to it you can do anything." Yep, that's the truth. It's that mindset. Get rid of the junk, the stuff you've heard from other people, the sooty thoughts floating around down there about your limitations, and there's no telling what can happen!

After all that bookwork, it was fun for her to practice flying. Bob said she caught on really quickly, and soon she was soaring all over the place. Of course, we had to pay for the instruction and the time in the plane, but Bob really enjoyed flying with her, and eventually, as Vicki's story unfolded, he donated a lot of time to her. I am so grateful for him and what he allowed himself to see in Vicki. He recognized who she was and trusted it. So did all those wonderful souls who saw the same thing and continued to work with her in the years to come. She did short-field landings in the local air show, visited cousins in a neighboring town, flew with Bob on short cross-countries, and then planned a long trip to Elizabeth's graduation from high school in North Carolina. The goals were expanding, and she was meeting them all. Soon, Vicki and Bob began thinking in a dramatic new direction, and a daring challenge began to take shape: a flight across the entire country. Vicki chose two cities that were as far apart as possible for her starting and ending points—Augusta, Maine, and San Diego, California—just to make it as demanding as possible. I can't say we, her parents, were excited about it, but Vicki sure was up for the challenge. It didn't take long for this giant-sized idea to eventually become a reality.

Now, to truly appreciate Vicki's modesty, to understand her humility, you must know that she never bragged to anyone about what she was doing. Only a very few of the students in her fifth-grade class knew anything about the flying, and they probably didn't believe it anyway. At the end of the school year, when the students had to stand in front of the class and share what they were doing for the summer, Vicki nonchalantly let it out: "Well, I'm planning and practicing for a flying trip across the country." I'm not sure anyone actually believed her.

The summer was filled with both planning and practicing. The walls of our long downstairs hallway were covered with flight maps from Augusta, Maine, to San Diego, California. Bob helped plan the overnight stops, but Vicki had to make decisions about where to land for fuel stops in between, calculating on her own how far she could safely fly. Bob was tough on her, but he wanted it that way because this trip could only be hers if she planned it herself, and indeed she did. There were lots of hours logged in the air, practice in emergency landings on grass runways, and practice landing in heavy air traffic in larger cities. Bob prepared her well, and Vicki accepted all the challenges with ease. Something big was in the works, and we had no idea just how big it was or would become.

I didn't do the flying to get well-known. I just wanted to get outside the box and fly! Some people might think the flying was all about me and ego, but I tell you I just wanted to show people, everyone, what they can do. And what is that? Anything! Come on, how cool to be a normal kid, and a girl, and be able to do that? So it was natural for the world to pay attention. Could I have somehow, somewhere created this?

So, it was the following September of 1993, at the start of her sixth-grade year, Vicki left her hometown in a Cessna 172, heading for Augusta, Maine, as planned, to start the trek with Bob across the country. Jim and I were along for the ride, so to speak. We flew to Maine separately to meet Vicki, bringing along her baseball glove, carefully packed in Jim's bags, so the two could play catch the night before she left on the big trip. We planned to follow the duo along their journey by commercial aircraft, meeting them at overnight sites so we could support Vicki.

Within a couple days of our arrival in Augusta, Vicki was asked to do an interview with an NBC reporter and television crew from Portland, Maine. I guess they were sent to see if this little-girl pilot was for real. I remember them quizzing Vicki as Jim and I walked away to allow her to answer all their questions. After all, we were not the pilots, and we knew Vicki could handle herself, but I guess we didn't know just *how* well until later.

It was the night before the trip was to begin. After dinner, Vicki and Jim played catch in the parking lot, then we checked our messages before retiring for the night. The desk was buzzing when Jim got there. It seems they had been trying to reach us for some time because there was a stack of important requests waiting—the most important being from *The Today Show*. They were sending a satellite dish, and Bryant Gumbel would be interviewing Vicki and Bob in the morning before they embarked on their journey. The dish was already on its way and would arrive at five in the morning! Their plan was to follow Vicki on the news each night as they made the trip across the country, and then interview her again in the studio in New York after the trip was completed. And that is what happened. In fact, all the news channels followed her as well, and invitations for radio interviews and television programs arrived each day as we all made our way to the other side of the country. It was quite amazing, and something that we certainly did not expect. Vicki handled it all like a pro. It was funny how it all happened—like it was meant to be.

The trip was to be completed in four days if all went well, and it did, but not without some bumps—the real bumps that made Vicki airsick, and the distractions of all the media along the way. Vicki had set some records: the youngest female to pilot a plane cross-country, the farthest distance, and the first east to west, which is tougher because she was flying against the wind. But it couldn't have turned out any better. All of it. Every single bit. I am so grateful for each moment.

We did fly in the back seat after her historic flight when she and Bob were invited to the Johnson Space Center. She was given special permission to land her plane at Ellington Field. There was no other way for us to enjoy the experience of being there with her because commercial aircraft are not permitted to land there, even to fly within the airspace surrounding this military installation. Jim and I were mesmerized as we actually, with our own eyes, saw our 11-year-old Vicki in total control of the aircraft. I mean, we knew it was all true, that she could pilot a plane, but to experience it first-hand was another story. Our lives were in her hands, our 11-year-old daughter's hands! So I guess trust goes both ways, doesn't it? Interesting.

You grateful? What about me? It was great! In case you don't know it, gratefulness is a really good thing to have—I mean being grateful for EVERYTHING. Oh, that record thing—what's a record anyway? Some silliness! Well, I got your attention! If there wasn't all this attention on what I did there, you wouldn't be reading this, would you? Hey, it's not about what I did while I was there, it's all about Who I am. Who you are. Do you get that? And look, flying isn't any big deal here. I move faster now and farther than you could ever imagine. Aaah, the limits of being there. Hmm. Are there limits?

Now, a secret from me. Actually, there are a few people who know this, but because of the nature of its content, I do not reveal this secret to many. I guess I am now: Many people have asked how it is that I got through Vicki's first flight— how I could stay so calm and not become a complete basket case. Well, aside from my prayers, my trust in God, and my confidence in Bob's abilities as an instructor pilot, I did something else that I hoped would bring me some extra, added immediate peace. I visited a psychic. Yes, I did. I had done that a number of times as my children grew, just to ask if there was anything I could do to help them along in their journeys. I never really pried into wanting to know everything, I just reached out to explore if I was missing something. I hoped to be the best mother I could be, and I thought this was a tool to use to help me do just that. I have since learned, without a doubt, that all answers lie within me, and it is up to me to listen to God whispering them in my heart, but at that time I needed a little help, and for this particular event in Vicki's life I needed as much assurance as I could get. I went for that 'children checkup', and at the very end of the session I informed the psychic that very soon my daughter would be piloting a single-engine plane across the country in four days' time. All I wanted to know was if she would safely complete the trip. He sat there with his eyes closed and paused as if living the adventure with her, then he replied, "Yes, she will be okay, but on the third day, she will be challenged as she never has been before. It will take almost everything from her, but she will make it." With that extra, added assurance, I released the question from my mind. I guess, for him, the energy of this event continued in its strength, for as we left the office, and before he moved on to the next waiting client, he turned to me and added, "They will be rolling out the red carpet for her. She just must remember that when it is time to leave, she must close the door and focus on what's at hand." I didn't quite know what he meant, but it wouldn't be long until I found out. I never shared any of this with Vicki. It was meant for me, her mother.

So, on the third day when her plane was hours late at Sky Harbor Airport in Phoenix, Arizona, I had a sense of what was going on, and I didn't panic. It was all proven to me after Vicki and Bob landed, and I saw Vicki's face as she left the cockpit. She was pale and weak; this day's journey had been a real ordeal for her. She had, indeed, been challenged to the max. For the first time on the trip, she brushed past the waiting reporters and festivities and headed for the restroom. She had encountered some really rough conditions on the last leg of this day; the plane had been bouncing wildly, and Vicki had become severely airsick. The morning she left Augusta the wind had been cold and strong, and after that first day she began showing signs of a cold, but now it looked like that slight cold had developed into an ear infection. The discomfort she was in was obvious. It all happened just as I had been told. And something else happened: We saw the tenacity, the perseverance, the strength of a little 11-year-old girl who held a message for the world. We witnessed her rising up and overcoming all obstacles to get that message out to humanity. Unbelievably, Vicki rallied, and before long came out of the restroom, and, with humility, addressed the waiting crowd, saying, "I knew it would be hard and it really was." And with that same modesty she finally smiled and showed once again who she was and what all people can be, if they choose it. Vicki later had the chance to go into more detail about that trip in a book she would later write.

On the last day of the flight Jim and I went to meet Vicki at Montgomery Field. As we rounded the corner and spotted the festivities, we could see stacks of satellite dishes, a long line of reporters, a platform holding city officials and dignitaries, well-wishers with cameras, even Shamu from Sea World—all there to welcome Vicki and Bob to San Diego, California. It was awesome! We knew we were part of something very special. I had the distinct feeling that Vicki had been made for this moment, and that we were meant to bring her into this world.

Yaah ... you think so? Okay, why do you think some people like that psychic can figure those things out? Could it be that they've already happened? I'm telling you that outside of there, time doesn't exist, and neither does space. I know, that's hard to wrap your head around. I'm just sayin'. But remember, the opportunity for choice, for possibility, is always open for you because you are creators in each moment. Everything is happening NOW!

As Vicki said in San Diego at the end of the trip, "We didn't think there would be this much ... people (motioning to the crowd) ... we thought it would just be a write-up in the newspaper or something." As it turned out, she was interviewed on radio shows as far away as Bogota, Columbia. Her journey made all the major television news channels and appeared in newspapers all over the world, even making the front page in the Arab news! Somehow it all fit into place; the way she carried herself during it all was natural to her—like she was born to do it. There definitely was also something about the way she came through to people—how they could relate to her. It was an unseen something that showed through her eyes and in the ease with which she handled herself under the pressures of questioning. The wit, the knowing—like a very old soul was showing itself through this little girl—and people, the reporters, the television viewers and all the radio listeners could sense it. She was real. What was happening to her was not orchestrated; everything floated seamlessly to her and through her. Vicki quickly gained a reputation on television as 'America's Sweetheart', and she was, for that short time in the public eye. There was something in her that caught the eye of the nation. Maybe today, amid all of the stories, hers would be lost, but it wasn't then—there was a destiny about it.

Look, you've all been many things. We just change places, like in a board game. For example, when you play "Monopoly" you get to pick a different token to use each time you play the game, and somebody else can pick the one you used in your last game. But this game is a giant one and very interesting with lots of layers to it. Just be what you picked, relax, listen to yourself, and hey, anything IS possible! I guess you are going to hear that a lot from me.

Vicki was not the only person being asked questions by reporters. Jim and I had our share as well, and it was challenging at times to know just how to respond. The thing is, when you say something to a reporter, you really have no idea how they will interpret it or change it around to somehow fit the story they choose to tell. It was always a little scary to pick up a paper and read in print what we supposedly said, or to see ourselves being interviewed on television. It's easy sometimes to sound less than bright, so I do have a bit of compassion for those in the public eye who may have gotten misunderstood in some way because of an interviewer's interpretation, well-meaning or not. Looking back on it now, even seeing actual interviews that we kept all these years, I too had a certain sense of calm that accompanied all the questioning. I don't know ... it really felt as though something very spiritual was happening around her trip and how the people were reacting to it and to her. My husband used to say that her plane was in God's hands, and it, along with Vicki in it, surely was. My prayer always included the image of an unseen hand gently placing the little Cessna gracefully on the ground at her destinations. There were many people praying for her during that time. The news stations followed her journey each night. It was incredible. This took place in 1993, before all news became so sensationalized. I think Vicki's story stood out because it held a sense of innocence and hopefulness. There was a message to it, and she delivered that message expertly. She told the people, "It doesn't matter what age you are, it's what you think, and how you feel about what you're doing. If you put your mind to it, you can do anything." And then she'd smile in humility as her spirit spoke and glimmered in her eyes. Everywhere we went, people were lifted up, and we could feel it. I distinctly remember sharing in an interview my wondering just how this experience of being able to rise above the earth and see it in such vastness would impact Vicki's life.

Wow, Mother, how did you know? It's like we sat down and set it up somewhere! Hmm. Where could that have been? Could we really just be spiritual beings living in a physical world? Could I have been flashing that spirit? Kids do that, you know. Take a look into a child's eyes and you can see it—the spirit. Hey, they are closer to where they came from than their parents. That's just how it is. Rising above the earth and seeing it all—you wondered how would that impact me? Wait a minute, how would that impact YOU?

After the completion of the flight, as well as surprise experiences Vicki was treated to as a result of the media coverage of her trip, our town of Meadville, Pennsylvania, held quite a homecoming for us. Vicki put our small community on the map all over the world, and they wanted to acknowledge it. Before she left on her cross-country flight, Vicki was named an ambassador for the city. She delivered promotional materials to each major airport in which she landed. She even managed to sneak in a plug for her town on a late night television show on which she appeared while in California. Those appearances and invitations kept us busy for some extra days, and while we were gone some key players in town arranged both a ceremony upon her landing at the airport and later a celebration at one of the local banks. It was all very special. A letter from Bill Clinton, President of the United States and First Lady Hillary Clinton was read at the ceremony, and Vicki received flowers, handshakes and lots of welcome-home smiles. You could feel the love, the support of relatives, friends, neighbors, teachers, her church family, and so many others who now knew Vicki through the news of her accomplishments. All were present to show their sincere pride. Later, at the more formal celebration at the bank, there were speeches, gifts, refreshments, even a small orchestra. Vicki was so happy to be home with her friends, and after the festivities they all sneaked around the corner to catch a movie together. I'm not sure what it was, but I know she was in seventh heaven!

It was all really nice, but the truth is, I was never impressed with myself. I was just *being* **... and that's the real truth.**

On her first day back at her elementary school, Vicki was

welcomed with student-created banners and a school-wide assembly in the gymnasium. It was a lovely gift to her, to us, and such an exciting and joyous occasion for everyone. The orchestra played, and the chorus sang a special song about flying free. Vicki was presented with a book on space from her teachers, and there were tons of smiles and lots of happiness in the air.

Vicki's days at her elementary school were filled with loving support, and the school community was proud of her accomplishments. The students were genuinely happy for her, and her teachers were exceptionally understanding and helpful, both during her flights and afterward as she continued to travel for other reasons. We were blessed that Vicki's teachers knew how important their role in her life was and that they responded to her needs with kindness, caring and encouragement.

After that assembly, and the rest of an exciting first day back at school, Vicki was looking forward to having some of her friends over to the house. She was separated from them for longer than she had imagined through all the unexpected events surrounding her cross-country trip and its aftermath. Her friends knew she was making the trip and would be gone for a week, but no one was prepared for the ensuing events that occurred once the trip began. The children saw Vicki on television each day and were even interviewed themselves for newspapers and television shows. Eventually her class even took a trip to Washington, D.C. with her. As a guest on one television show, Vicki was expected to receive an invitation to visit the White House, but she extended that invitation by asking to include her entire class in the experience. And so it happened that they all toured the White House, met with astronaut John Glenn, visited Arlington National Cemetery, and experienced other memorable moments together.

Back to the first day home. Word got around during the day that some of the kids were going to Vicki's house after school. For some reason I was not in town at the time. At first, a group of Vicki's friends arrived, and eventually, the whole class. Vicki frantically called her dad at work and said, "Dad, don't get mad, but the whole class is here! Could you bring home some pizzas for us?" One of the lovely advantages of living in a small town is that everything is so close. Our children could walk to school, and my husband was within walking distance of his office. So before long, Jim came home with four large pizzas and sodas, and the party outside our backdoor went on. That was another really great event. Something else happened that day, something else quite exceptional. There was a little girl, a member of the class, who heard about the plans and who came along to the gathering. Some of the other students questioned her, "Why are *you* here? You're not her friend; you weren't invited!" Vicki heard what happened, and she stepped in, "Hey, wait, she's my friend, too! Of course she should be here!" So that afternoon became a memorable experience for everyone. We have pictures to prove it! But the really wonderful thing happened years later, after Vicki left this plane of existence. That grown-up little girl whom Vicki rescued wrote us a sincere letter recalling that day and just how much that gesture from Vicki had meant to her. Its kindness stayed in her heart and will remain with her for a lifetime, and so will *her* kindness in sharing her remembrance with us. Isn't that something—to think how words of kindness, once expressed, live on.

Now that's some big stuff, there. Positive words—they do live on, you know—they don't go away. After they come out of your mouth they float around, and people can pick them up and keep them for a long time, but so do the negative ones. Yep, once they come out, they're floatin' around out there too, where you think nothing is but empty space. Guess again. And it happens just the same even if you think them. I told you that you were awesome,

remember?

Flight 2 developed as a natural extension of Flight 1. After Vicki's flight across the United States, reporters immediately started asking her, "What's next, Vicki? What's next?" It was as if what she had already done wasn't enough, but you know, that's how reporters are. Besides, Vicki always continued to expand her goals anyway. She loved challenges, and she pushed the envelope once again when she finally answered them with, "I think I'll do something with the Atlantic, like fly over it!" And she did that, too.

It was decided that she would need a new instructor because Bob wasn't really for the idea, for safety reasons. If they made the trip together he would only be comfortable in a twin engine airplane, and that meant Vicki would have to learn to fly one. True, the actual flying time would be shorter, and the trip easier once that was accomplished, but taking everything into consideration, it didn't seem as challenging to Vicki, and all the preparation involved in learning and mastering the piloting of a twin-engine airplane didn't appeal to her. She knew how to pilot a single-engine aircraft, but she would have to find a way to stop for refueling; there are no fuel stops to be made in the middle of the Atlantic! Here is where Stan Parkins came in. We met Stan on one of Vicki's overnight stops and developed a fast friendship with him—more on Stan later. Stan knew Curt Arnspiger, who ferried planes across the Atlantic by island-hopping from Canada to Greenland to Iceland and over into Europe. He had been doing this for some time as a well-paying hobby, so to speak, ferrying single-engine airplanes to buyers in Eastern European countries. He was the contact—the perfect person for the job. Curt enthusiastically agreed to be Vicki's instructor! It is still incredible to me how the right person, at the right time, can come into your life. Vicki certainly had more than her fair share of them. But Curt, a successful businessman, didn't have an instructor's license, which he would need in order to accompany Vicki. So, with his enthusiasm for adventure, he began the process to get one, which by the way, didn't come through for him until the very day before the trip was to start!

In the meantime, Vicki had to train on a new plane, one with a more powerful engine, a Cessna 210. It was a new challenge, one that she met and mastered. Because that second trip was pretty monumental, we all decided that the plane should have a name. The plane itself was purchased with the plan that it would be sold over in Europe after the trip to recoup some of the initial investment, and eventually that did happen. So, there was the question of the name. Vicki's choice was *Murphy*, but that didn't describe the purpose of this next journey. Lots of ideas for possible names were discussed, but we all settled on *Harmony*. It symbolized a working together, a blending of sound, and everything living together in peace. That seemed right to us, and to Vicki, for she taught us to know that she would never do or say anything that deep down wasn't right to her.

As plans for the Atlantic crossing progressed I read the booklet all pilots must read before attempting such a risky flight in a single-engine aircraft. It was daunting. Many pilots are lost each year in North Atlantic icy waters. Vicki had read the material and was well aware of all possibilities. When I questioned her about her feelings, asking if she was fearful, she calmly explained to me, "Everyone thinks differently." Her response took me back to the time she uttered the words, "Whose choice is it, Mother?" These words too, gave me pause. Out of the mouths of babes . . . .

Hey, wasn't that the name of a movie about a pig? You don't have to understand me or agree. Just know that both our thoughts exist: yours and mine.

She took many reporters and cameramen up into the skies in

Harmony, and they all marveled at her skill. She worked with some very experienced flight instructors in Ohio while training for her Atlantic trip. Jim drove her to them on the weekends so she could practice and make plans for the crossing. Mike Reilly and Dick Willis worked with her at Eddie Rickenbacker Airfield in Columbus, Ohio. The airstrip was ideal because it had a three-mile runway that allowed Vicki to practice touching down and landing twice each go around. The 210 had a much more powerful engine, and she needed to develop control over it to safely land. One of the instructors was a DC10 captain and had experience island-hopping in single engine aircraft to Europe. Both of them willingly shared what they knew to assist Vicki in the planning. This trip could not happen without the benefit of their expertise, just as the first trip was made possible by Bob's proficiencies and his willingness to share it all with Vicki. These super skilled, risk-taking individuals are to be admired. They belong to a fraternity all their own, and it is pretty tough to earn your way in, but Vicki did when she was just twelve. So, with the assistance of each of these outstanding and generous fliers, the bar was raised for Vicki and she responded by expanding herself to reach it.

You all have them, too—people who step into your life to assist you in some way. They're all around you; they are your runners. You never know who they might be or how you might meet them, or how they might help you, or what the help might look like. It might not even be just the 'good stuff' they offer you, either. What doesn't feel so good now just might turn into something helpful to you in the long run. Interesting, huh?

I like that expanding part ... expanding ... opening up your thinking to new possibilities. Is that possible—for you, I mean? There are a whole lot of possibilities out there, as many as you can think of. And more! Are you afraid of something? No fear—that's the message! Hmm ... harmony. Maybe that's what I was spreading while I was flying.

Okay, back to Stan and another secret revealed! Vicki actually started driving a beautiful blue Corvette on the road when she was just twelve. Yes, it's true! That opportunity was supplied by an angel named Stan. An angel he was, and is. Stan saw Vicki on the news and made sure he was at one of her overnight stops on the cross-country flight. He heard her remark impatiently, "My father doesn't know how to pick out peaches. He bought them for me for the trip and days later, they're still rocks!" Well, once Stan heard Vicki's comments, he arrived at our hotel with some ripe peaches, along with pilot goodies for the road. We opened our hotel door to him, but he opened the door to our hearts. The following morning he became part of the early morning send-off crew, along with one of his Sunday School students, Kaylyn, who offered Vicki the gift of a tiny Bible to place in the pocket of her flight suit. Stan remained a very special friend to our whole family for years until he passed into the next life. He was instrumental in connecting Vicki with that second group of instructors for her flight across the Atlantic. Stan made sure she took a glider lesson, attempted to teach her to ski, and introduced Vicki to skydiving, a sport which she thoroughly enjoyed later in her life. Vicki admired how Stan, a skilled pilot himself, made everything look so easy. Well, Vicki kind of did that in her own way, too, I guess. Vicki and Stan: kindred spirits. I imagine they are flying around on some new adventures together wherever they are.

Angels among you ... ☺ ☺

The Atlantic trip would be an island-hopping adventure. It was to begin with Vicki and Curt flying the Cessna 210 from Meadville, Pennsylvania, to Augusta, Maine, where their Atlantic crossing would officially begin with a send-off from the Maine State Airport.

They would continue on to Goose Bay, Canada, staying overnight. The next day it was on to Narsarsuaq, Greenland, and ending that day's trip in Reykjavik, Iceland, where Jim and I would meet them. The following day was to mark the actual crossing with a landing in Glasgow, Scotland, then on to Biggin Hill Airport in England. In the days to follow, Vicki would continue on to airports in France and Germany. After flying commercially from Iceland to Scotland to meet Vicki in Glasgow, we would follow along the rest of her travel itinerary by car.

If someone had seen Vicki's interview on television, the one she gave after the Atlantic flight filmed at the harbor in New York City on the United States Naval carrier, *Entrepid*, they would have seen a calm and composed young female pilot. That is what Vicki was. She had a way of dismissing fears, putting them into perspective. She had an attitude that didn't allow her to give power to anything that would prevent her from living in the moment. I guess kids can sometimes be that way in their innocence, but with Vicki, there was a maturity level that caused her to rise above fear.

She and Curt went through some threatening icing conditions on the leg between Goose Bay, Canada, and Narsarsuaq, Greenland, and had to eventually end up flying about 500 feet above the ocean to avoid the plane crashing into the frigid waters under the weight of ice on the wings. Vicki took it in stride, landing in Greenland before a crowd of Innuit children carrying signs announcing her arrival.

By the way, I recently read an article that stated the airport at Narsarsuaq is considered one of the most difficult airports in the world in which to land. I've indicated that these pilots deal with many danger-filled situations, and they don't flinch. Neither did Vicki. She also didn't say much about the leg between Glasgow, Scotland, and London, England, when they were forced to fly higher than expected to avoid other icing conditions, and she experienced light-headedness due to the lack of extra oxygen in the small plane. But she never complained about anything. If we thought at all that she wasn't at the controls, that false notion was dashed when we saw her actual cross-wind landing in Glasgow, Scotland. It is preserved for all to see because Curt was holding a camera for *Dateline* in his hands and merely watched and filmed Vicki as she set the plane down, the wind blowing strong enough to set the grass on its side. When she landed in the airport near Fismes, France, we heard her ask a very surprised tower for permission to use, not the paved runway, the normal pilot's choice, but instead, the grass runway next to it, a much more challenging landing option. She was used to grass runways from practicing on them during her training with Bob. She seemed to have no fear, and she never chose to take the easy way out.

Darned right. I didn't even use the auto-pilot! I never did take the easy way out. Maybe some of you might think so, now, because of the choice I made to leave the earth 'reality', but if you do, you're thinking too much, and that's okay. You'll understand sometime, someday. Maybe.

Try to understand what it was like twenty-plus years ago. Today, the media, in all aspects, is reporting all kinds of odd news, from the bizarre to the contrived, with some truth smattered inside. It's all about shock and awe today, or at least that's how it seems to me. The story of Vicki's first flight caught the attention of the NBC news channel right before she took off from Augusta, Maine, and they started the ball rolling with daily coverage, beginning with that live interview with Bryant Gumbel just prior to take-off. I guess the innocence of her story had wide-spread appeal. As I've said before, she caught the public's attention, and many people followed the daily reports of her progress on the news each night, some even showing up at the airports where she landed, to meet her. The coverage and the crowds increased as she made her way west. It was like something—some kind of force—helped it all happen. I don't know. Lifetime movies were just starting then, and soon after Vicki's flights, a producer wanted to make a movie of her story, but we didn't think it was appropriate. Another star personality expressed interest in making a movie, but the characters would have to be altered to allow them to become more 'story-worthy'. We could never understand why the true account was not quite interesting enough for them. We decided that we could never damage the lives of people whom we loved and cared about just for the entertainment value of a movie, so we passed on that one as well.

Looking back on it now, it feels to me that there was a moment in our country's history when the media's focus really changed, and it happened shortly after Vicki landed in Europe. O.J. Simpson made his escape in a white Ford Bronco, and humanity's focus shifted. Vicki's Atlantic crossing story was held in limbo from airing on *Dateline* because of its lack of sensationalism. The story eventually ran, but it did so after the fascination with the O.J. story died down for a bit.

As Vicki's parents, we were determined to allow her story to be used only in a truthful and positive manner, so we settled on allowing a book about Vicki's flights to be written for children. We were approached by several people interested in working on that book, but we quickly settled on Dan Gutman, a wonderful man, a sportswriter of children's books, who contacted us after seeing a picture of a Cubs' emblem on Vicki's bedroom wall in a picture included in a feature story for The New York Times. He felt drawn to Vicki because of their shared interest in baseball. It became a fine collaboration, with him generously acknowledging Vicki as co-author. *Taking Flight: My Story by Vicki Van Meter,* was recognized and recommended for reading by librarians at the time, though it wasn't a bestseller. But it didn't have to be; it was the truth.

Speaking of truth, we all must find our own, and it takes time, or not! I knew one truth that I talked a lot about in my speeches: Anything Is Possible! I knew it deep down when I was there, and guess what? Deep down you know it, too! You know a lot of things deep down. Truth is speaking to you all the time. You just have to be still, ignore the distractions, and clear out all the junk inside your head to hear it. And believe me, that is possible, too!

As Vicki journeyed through her flying adventures, it was customary for Jim to keep track of all the articles, letters and memorabilia she gathered along the way. His managerial skills stepped forward as he took charge of all her invitations to speak, to give interviews on radio and television, and to make appearances. He was great at that. He always tried to be kind to everyone who contacted him about Vicki. We felt that it was an honor to be asked to do such things, and Vicki wanted to participate in all of those opportunities. She was humbled by it. We also felt that the messages she was giving were good ones, and we saw their impact on the people who gathered around her during her flights. If Jim had not been a wise manager and preserver of Vicki's history, we would not have in our possession such an accurate accounting of all the events surrounding her achievements. Jim carefully laminated everything and stored it all neatly away along with photos, certificates and videos. It's almost like he knew they were very important to keep. Our children thought he was obsessed, and maybe it might have looked that way to them, but now I would bet they are glad we have every single bit of everything about Vicki. Now I think we'd agree there was a reason for it to happen.

It didn't bother me. I knew he was doing it, but when he asked me to look at the stuff, I didn't want to see it. I mean, I was there when it happened—I lived it! No need to watch that play. You know, life is not a dress rehearsal! I must say that I'm glad now for all of it because it helps you, Mother, get my points across from this side. I guess it makes me come alive to you guys. Whoa! Hey, what am I sayin'? I am alive! At least I am here!

There were two components to Vicki's eventual success in reaching the world stage. Of course, she appeared to be a flying prodigy, having a natural-born aptitude and ability in that arena. It was as though she had come into this life having done it all before. The comparison to Amelia Earhart was often made. In some ways she even looked like her. Jim read a book on Amelia and was taken with so many details of her life that seemed to parallel Vicki's. At the time of Vicki's Atlantic flight, the papers reported that Vicki was following Amelia's flight path across the Atlantic. That wasn't exactly true, but there was something else that was: Vicki's first trip in a single-engine airplane across the Atlantic was as a passenger just as Amelia's had been.

Vicki made a pre-trip to Iceland along with her instructor for the purpose of determining if she really desired to do it all again, piloting the airplane herself. Amelia's notoriety came as a result of just being a passenger on that flight across the Atlantic. When Vicki landed in San Diego after her flight across America, a representative who presented her with a key to the city introduced her saying, "Welcome, Amelia! Oh, I mean, Vicki!" When you think about it, it is interesting to note the mystery surrounding Amelia's disappearance on her flight around the world—and Vicki's 'disappearance' from this earth. They made their marks and launched messages of possibility, especially for women, and then they left.

The man doesn't know how right he was, does he ... or was he? Interesting!

Another component—and this, too, bears a similarity to Amelia—is that Vicki was well equipped to reach people through her communication skills. Jim and I saw it first-hand as the journey began. As Jim and I flew on that commercial plane to Augusta, Maine we had no idea what lay ahead. From our perspective, Vicki was just following through with a goal. She planned to begin her trip at the farthest distance in the east: Augusta, Maine, a city that, coincidentally, Amelia had once used as a starting point, and to end it in San Diego, California, the farthest distance in the west. All the fuel stops and major overnight destinations in-between were carefully planned, too. Vicki's history with attending flight school training and flying the Cessna 150 in other exploits close to our town made the local news. It was an interesting and unusual story happening in our small town. Her reason for making the trip was not for the notoriety, it was for the satisfaction of achieving her goal. She didn't need anything more than that, as evidenced by her choice to toss her baseball glove into her dad's suitcase so she and her father could play catch between flights. There were no expectations of what was to come. It was all unexpected and sort of miraculous.

The media frenzy started with that interview in Augusta before her first scheduled flight. I remember when the reporter asked Vicki her first question on the tarmac of the airport; she looked at us, and Jim and I made a choice right then and there. She would handle this on her own, and that's the way she wanted it. We had no intention of interfering, so we slipped away as Vicki took control. We could see them intently talking as we paced around wondering what she was saying, but we weren't concerned because it looked as if she was taking charge, and we could feel her confidence. That's how it started, and that's how it continued. Vicki always said whatever she wanted to say. and she did it with intelligence, calm and flair. Nobody ever told her to say something; what she said was always her decision, and how she handled it all was quite remarkable, and everyone knew it. I guess the story resulting from that interview was the catalyst for all the news coverage to come as she piloted the Cessna across the country.

Eventually, she went on television shows and continued to sparkle and impress. Before guests emerge on the set of a talk show, they are interviewed just to make sure things will go smoothly, especially when children are involved. Well, the prep people never had to stay very long after they met Vicki. As a result, her reputation for a good interview expanded her invitations, each one being an opportunity to shine. On one occasion, when her sister Elizabeth was in acting school, she had the opportunity to accompany Vicki and me on a trip to Los Angeles when Vicki was scheduled to be on *The Tonight Show with Jay Leno*. After having the opportunity of meeting a very famous comedian who was also Jay's guest that night, Elizabeth and I were seated in the green room before Vicki was to make her appearance. Vicki was as calm as could be, and her sister turned to me and frustratingly asked, "How can she do it? She isn't even nervous or anything!" I assured her that this was Vicki's style. She was present and truthful; she didn't have to be nervous.

And speaking of that famous comedian. let me share a great story that I can never forget. That celebrity was Whoopi Goldberg, and Vicki, Elizabeth and I had the unexpected privilege of meeting her that day before *The Tonight Show with Jay Leno* began taping. Elizabeth and I were a bit star-struck, but Vicki was cool as we were led to Whoopi's dressing room door to meet with her privately. Pleasantries were exchanged, and I imagine Whoopi noticed our excitement at meeting someone so famous as herself. It is what she did next that showed the kindness of her heart. I remember that after she and Vicki briefly spoke, she raised her hand to gently peel the sparkling star off the dressing room door that held her name, and she graciously handed it to Vicki, saying, "You're the real star, Vicki!"

I recall the energy of that moment and the warmth of a mother's love in our embrace after it. That star has always been among Vicki's favorite mementos.

Being at the right place at the right time is no coincidence. There are no coincidences. Do you know that?

During her cross-country flight, Jim and I got the extent of how incredible this journey with Vicki had become. We were seated on the plane when we noticed a man reading from an open newspaper upon which Vicki's picture was spread across the front page. It was pretty wild! The pace, the scope of outreach, just continued from there. It was to become a whirlwind for two years: the first flight, shows, appearances, training for the second flight, the second flight, still more speeches, shows, and appearances. Although we were in the background, we, her parents, were always a part of it, being witness to the impact she was having on the world's stage. As Jim worked at his job, many times I accompanied Vicki to events. She sure made our lives full and fascinating for a number of years. I can't possibly name all the opportunities she had to speak: some at private companies, some at NASA facilities, some at school assemblies. The accolades given to her were incredible. She even won an ESPN Arete Award for Superlative Courage in Sports, along with Evander Holyfield, the boxer. Many of those honors represented a recognition of her achievement due to her age and being a girl. She had a lot to say about possibility. That point can't be denied. She was an advocate for kids, and girls, but her message was also ageless. Her feats were included in many magazines and children's school books. I taught school years later, and in my students' reader was a story about Vicki. Her younger cousin was shocked and moved to laughter when he came across a reading passage about her on one of his end-of-grade standardized reading tests! He got those questions right!

It doesn't matter what age you are or what your body looks like, you are ageless, you are spirit! Possibility—that's what it's all about! Hey, those Arete Awards were pretty interesting. Courage in sports ... hmm. Why did that one happen? Like I've said before, it's a game you're in there in the world—the real Game of Life! It takes courage to live your life—all of it—to face your fears. You and I know there have been plenty of challenges, things that were tough for you, and you got through it! You've done that before, other times, other places, and obviously you enjoyed it all or got something from it because you wanted to come back and do it all again! You are all just as courageous as you think I was. Living without fear—maybe that's what I was trying to help you see.

Vicki was only 12 when she was first asked to give those major speeches to large groups of people. She could handle herself brilliantly 'on the fly' when asked questions by reporters or other inquiring minds, but I knew she could use a little assistance in putting her thoughts and ideas together when planning a much longer speech to present before a crowd. I would talk with her about what she wanted to say, and I tried to be open to understanding her feelings and opinions about things. I also attempted to build upon comments she already offered to the public in her interviews. The process became a collaborative effort between us. I hasten to add here, it was Vicki who then delivered all those words in her own style and in her own way without coaching from me. She would never say anything she did not want to say, and she was genuine in her presentation. There was nothing pretentious about her. She was never boastful; she was just real, and everyone could sense it. I would usually make an outline of important points for her, based on our talks and my observations, and she had latitude in adding or subtracting whatever she chose to as she gave her speech. I felt that in this amazing story of our lives it was my part to help Vicki speak the truth of who she was. I didn't yet see the whole picture, but I had a sense of it, and underneath it all, think we both knew it.

Boy, did you get that one right, Mother! Get a load of* this *collaboration! Actually, people there are involved in collaborations of all kinds. There are other worlds, other dimensions 'living' right beside you. I'm trying to tell you that once you make room in your head to imagine it, well, everything looks a lot different there in your world! It's your choice to believe it, or not. It's always your choice.

We felt deeply honored when Vicki was asked to speak before the Pennsylvania State Senate, an invitation that is rarely made to anyone outside the chambers, let alone a 12-year-old girl. The poise with which she made that speech impressed not only the senators, but her parents, as well. Vicki was amazing; she had the ability to draw people in wherever and to whomever she spoke. There was a special story behind her trip to France, and Pennsylvania was a part of it. In World War II, soldiers from our town in Pennsylvania liberated the small French town of Fismes, located in champagne country about 75 miles northeast of Paris. Needless to say, there is a deep and continued feeling of gratitude flowing from this lovely little town to the citizens of Pennsylvania. Vicki's Atlantic crossing happened to coincide with festivities surrounding the 50th anniversary of the D-Day Landing on the beaches of Normandy, when troops of American soldiers arrived to join forces to help liberate France from the German armies. As part of that celebration, a bridge in Fismes was being re-dedicated to soldiers from our town of Meadville. Our city created a special plaque as a gift for Vicki to deliver, remembering that company of hometown soldiers who liberated the town. It was meant to commemorate the friendship of the two sister cities and was to be placed on the bridge where the final battle for the city had taken place and where victory was won. Vicki would be in Paris as one of the stops on her continued trip through Europe, so it seemed logical that she should deliver the heavy bronze plaque, which she carried all the way across the Atlantic in her little airplane. It was truly an honor for her to do so and for us to be a part of it.

Vicki was asked to report to the Senate about her Atlantic crossing and the trip to Fismes. She was engaging, mature beyond her years; her humor bubbled out, and she captured a lot of hearts that day. A year later, when she worked as a page in the Pennsylvania House of Representatives, the chamber recognized her by giving her a long-lasting standing ovation. To this day, when I see the event replayed on a tape that Jim saved, it gives me chills, and I can't help but tear up. Vicki took it all in stride, responding with grace and wit, as usual.

Again, I tell you, I was never impressed with what I did or said. Hey, you don't come to the game to impress. If you try to do that, well, you're off track. You come to play, and while you're playing, you learn, and you teach. The trouble is, you don't know for sure what it is you're there for when you're there, but if you relax and do that clearing of junk in your head, your mind will open and then you can hear something. You might get it, or not. Not to worry; it's all okay! See, you've got time, the game never ends. It just IS. There's that time thing again, I mean lack of it! Looking at my life now, I remember I always did like France. Maybe I played there before, when I was BEING human, or do I mean when I was a human BEING? Interesting . . . .

It amazed us just how far word of Vicki's feats spread during her flying adventures. In the beginning, images of this little-girl pilot began appearing in all the media, and by the time the trip was completed, the news had filtered out into the world. People sent us letters with copies of news articles and reports of her on their television news stations in Japan, Australia, New Guinea, South

America, Europe, even the Arab countries. It was equally amazing to eventually see her picture in one particular magazine along with images of Mother Theresa, Hillary Clinton, and other famous people who have conquered great obstacles in their lives. It continued to fascinate us to see it all happen, may I say, electrically; she was riding some kind of positive current making its way around the world. It wasn't just about the accomplishments at her young age, but something in her presence that caught people's attention. On her second flight she chose to spread herself even farther by actually flying to other countries. To be recognized, to hold the interest, the awareness of the world, even for a moment, is a major and thought-provoking event in anyone's life.

Yep, it was quite an opportunity to be able to reach people there on such a wide scale, and from this side, too. Maybe that's what I'm doing, now—just flying even farther. Can you imagine the worlds I can see now? Ohhh, the possibilities! That's all I'm sayin'. Think what you want, but it's more exciting to use your imagination!

Another not-too-well-known fact is that Vicki was close to completing plans on her next goal: a world flight. She wanted to fly around the world, and she didn't want to fly to big cities with lots of people and fanfare. Instead, she would fly around the world for kids—visiting small villages, taking them computers and other educational materials. Vicki related so well to children wherever she went, and she looked forward to flying to unexpected places. There was an instructor lined up to accompany her on this monumental undertaking. I was scheduled to fly periodically to meet her in major cities so I could tutor her in her school work.

Vicki caught the attention of someone who saw the potential good in an endeavor such as this, and soon people were working to help bring this giant idea into reality. Some major sponsors were lining up, waiting to make it all happen. This flight, and the good it would do in so many ways, held the makings of an epic adventure that could impact children all over the world. The companies involved wanted to support Vicki's goals, but their interest also lay in benefiting young people by associating the flight with an educational program that would allow kids in schools across our country and other countries to follow her trip through newspapers and online services. Remember, this was in 1994, at the beginning of the implementation of computers into everyday life. Vicki's flight held the potential of connecting children around the world through the educational process. There would also be opportunities for humanitarian service, as well as many other exciting, expanding ideas to be explored. Vicki was the one to make it happen. She had proven herself through her accomplishments, and through her ability to communicate. She had captured the attention of the world. Here, in her own words and with her own pen, she spells it out in a statement she wrote back in 1994:

I enjoy flying and look forward to the excitement of a World Flight 1995 challenge. But my main reason for wanting to make this flight is not to achieve a personal goal. I want to fly for a higher purpose. My past flights have seemed to become an inspiration for people of all ages. On this flight, I would like to represent the youth of this country and the world and encourage them to strive to give their best to our planet. Young people can do important things, too. Even though "we're" young our ideas can be big and helpful. "We" can act as a force for good in this world and can make a difference in a big way. I believe that anything is possible for each one of us if we put our minds to it.

Vicki

Things were moving forward on the plans for World Flight 1995, and the future looked bright. This was Vicki's way to help make good things happen in this world, just as she had shared with other kids in speeches she had given over the last year, encouraging them to realize the many opportunities that are waiting for them to contribute to the planet. There were adults waiting to help make her vision unfold; they, too, were connected to her and knew the good that could be achieved by this next giant endeavor. Vicki didn't want to disclose the plan to the public until it was totally complete. The prospects were exciting, to say the least, and I believe she was looking forward to it all. You could see it in her eyes.

Okay, we'll see what happens next, or what doesn't happen next. What shall we see? We shall see what we shall see!

Conflict

Maybe, if we dared to look inside someone else,

we'd see ourselves.

The little lantern watched the people dance and smile and play,
And longed to laugh along with them and have a 'normal' day.
So it tried to dim its light so all the people could see
That the lantern was just the same as them ... filled with all possibility!

At first it was a little game the lantern thought it could play,
But transforming darkness into light became tougher each day.
The little lantern was weakening and it began to fear
That it would not be long before all its light would disappear.

And so it was that Vicki moved on from her experience at the elementary school to the only junior high school in our little town. She left the nurturing and nourishing atmosphere of her supportive K-6 elementary school and entered a whole new world. All the elementary schools from across the entire town merged into one.

Junior high: one of the most trying times in a growing and developing soul's life. In a small town it is easy for a student to meet someone new from a different school through sporting activities and other kinds of common pursuits, but it's not as probable there would be one student with whom the entire school, grades seven through nine, would be familiar. Well, there was one: Vicki. She wasn't acquainted with each one personally, but they all thought they knew *her*, having read about her in the papers and seen her on television, and that included all the teachers, many of whom had children around the same age as Vicki.

All children at this age are bound to have some self-esteem issues; this is natural. Some acting out due to this is understandable, but because of Vicki's unique situation and the jealousy it seemed to engender in some of her new classmates, she received more than her fair share of—dare I say—abuse, from the school community, which we have grown to know set the stage for much of the conflict that became part of her life.

Vicki's heart's desire was to be like everyone else, to fit in, and she tried very hard to do just that. But she wasn't just like everyone else, and for that matter, who is? At that age young people are generally not yet comfortable with their uniqueness. We are all different, and eventually we grow to see that as a good thing, but it takes time for the recognition to come. Vicki knew that because of the notoriety she had received there would be an adjustment time for the students at the school to 'get over it'; to know that she was just normal like they were. She instinctively knew that she must wait for that to happen. She was giving them time and proceeding with caution. She tried to avoid situations that might lead to unexpected and unwanted attention. It didn't take her long to know that standing in the courtyard with the rest of her friends, waiting for the doors to open before the bell rang, was not a safe place. Invariably, someone would yell something for everyone to hear like, "Hey Vicki, can you fly off the building for us?" She kept so many of those hurtful moments to herself, but we eventually learned about some of them.

In those first days, there were some students who asked for her autograph, and she tried to brush it off, not wanting to make a big deal of it. One day, an older student whose parent was a teacher at the school asked her to sign a picture of herself for him. A long-time friend advised, "Vicki, go ahead, they just want your autograph." She finally gave in and signed the picture. Later, as she passed his open locker, she saw the picture of herself hanging there with a knife through it. She quickly learned she didn't know whom to trust.

My old friends were having a hard time feeling accepted, too. I don't blame them, it's just that it could have been a bit more pleasant if—hey, wait a minute. They each had their issues, and it's all okay, isn't it?

Up to this point in her life, Vicki acted from a pure kind of place; unencumbered and free. She seemed to just be who she was. It shown in her eyes, it glowed in her being, it reflected to everyone around her. She made it all look so easy. Her carefree way of being was contagious. It was like she didn't capture and hold in her any of the negative. If she did, the power in her was able to overcome that which was the opposite of who she was being. Vicki was born with some special kind of resiliency. It's hard to explain, but all you would have to do is to watch her in a television interview to feel who she was inside. Then you would know. At least it used to be that way; things were beginning to change now.

There have been some cleverly made movies where something magical happens and suddenly one person finds themselves in another person's body. You know the ones. In this new movie of Vicki's life, it was she who seemed able to change herself. Well, it wasn't as if the kids around Vicki weren't acting their age, it was as if there was an older person in Vicki's body. When she found herself in the capacity of doing anything connected with flying, she was real, living in her potential, and when she found herself among her peers, she, like a chameleon, could switch energies to become like them. She wanted to prove she was just like them and to enjoy those kid kinds of experiences. At least, that's what it seemed was happening. Actually, as I think of it now, that makes her sort of ageless, doesn't it?

Bingo! Newsflash: YOU ARE AGELESS, TOO! Could I have been there observing things at this point? Maybe? You really don't know, do you? That's okay, you don't have to. Can't say I got it all myself then either. That's just how it is.

During that first year of Vicki's junior high our family went through a major crisis. My mother almost died and was in the intensive care unit of a major hospital for months. Although we lived distances apart, my two brothers, two sisters and I took turns traveling separately to be with her each day until she was in the clear. A day did not go by that someone was not there in that intensive care room with her. For days at a time we kept vigil over her, never leaving her alone until she was on solid ground. Even when I was not physically there with her, my mind was on my mother as Vicki began and lived through those early months at her new school. Invitations, appearances and speeches continued to come, too.

On weekends, once a month, she and her father continued to drive to Ohio to work with her instructors, preparing for Vicki Van Meter's World Flight 1995, which would take place the following year. She never bragged about what she was doing, never told anyone about the flight plan. She was trying to exist in the difficult environment at the junior high where she learned that potential problems were avoided by staying away from all crowds. We tried to assist her with that strategy. Her day would begin with Jim dropping her off at school on his way to work at just the right moment, after all the students were inside, out of the halls and in their homerooms in the building. Just before the second bell rang, Vicki would slip in the closest door to her homeroom, quickly get her books from her locker and pass through the door, trying to make it to her seat before the final bell rang. Most of the time she made it, but if she was not in her seat before the bell, she would receive a tardy from the teacher. It was a rule. She could be inside the door about to sit down and the teacher would still issue the tardy.

Eventually, Vicki received detentions for her tardies. We always wondered why it was that this teacher, whose own children were about the ages of ours, and whom we knew, or a counselor, or anyone else in administration never had a conversation with Vicki or with us to try and understand what was going on in her world. Perhaps that may have helped the situation, and an understanding of some kind could have been reached. I know there must be rules, but rules without compassion can be damaging. Vicki always insisted that we not go to the school and get involved—that it would only make things worse. I knew that was a possibility. She would never ask for any special favors, and we didn't want that either, just some understanding.

Now, don't get me wrong, there were some nice teachers; there were some okay teachers, but all it takes is one to change

everything either way. You'd think adults would know better, but they don't always get it either. They're still learning, too, about that ego thing and working to overcoming it or not. Ego: the human way of thinking about self; the it's-all-about-me-and-my-power attitude. So, understanding—I guess it can go both ways.

When Vicki did her flying, we had such an outpouring of support from our family, our church, our community—from people all over the country and around the world. It is a fantastic thing to ride upon the waves of that energy. What a beautiful experience! But, also traveling along with us, underneath the highs, was some negative energy. There were those who looked upon Vicki's accomplishments as something to be judged. I remember sitting in a restaurant when I heard the comment of a respected person in town, uttered for me to hear, "Well, with all that Vicki has done, there's nowhere for her to go but down."

I also remember a friend sharing with me that someone whom I didn't even know professed to be an expert on our family's business, and finally declared that we were 'stuck up'. To her credit, my friend set the woman straight on her 'facts'. As an adult it was challenging to deflect this negative energy. I can only imagine what Vicki went through on a daily basis at school trying to live her life as a regular person. Everyone is entitled to an opinion, but I wonder if some people are aware how damaging what they say can be. Through it all, I learned to have some compassion for those on the world stage who find themselves maligned, misjudged. Perhaps it is judgment that is at the core of the problem; judgment and jealousy.

Dang, you people can be so mean to each other! Jealousy is an ugly thing, especially when it comes from an adult. They just have a different way of showing it. Little kids don't know anything about jealousy, they learn it from someone. Ahemmm ... are you listening, grown-ups?

Jealousy, envy—they're just more silliness. Look, you're all connected, like one big body, and if something good happens to someone, it's happening to everyone. It's happening to you, too, if you'd let yourself feel it!

Stay with me on this one: Let's say YOU are a body. Well, you do have one, don't you? That's why I'm using this physical analogy. Okay, you've got lots of parts on that body. Now, say you get your nails done and they are lookin' good or your hair gets cut and it looks really cool. The whole body feels great because of that happening, right? The other parts aren't holding back from feeling good about it, too! It's kind of like that.

Too bad some people can't let themselves feel that kind of whole-body joy while they are there. So much sadness comes from not getting that one. I tell you, this can be eradicated!

During Vicki's sixth grade year, she spoke at many NASA facilities, including Space Camp, and each time represented herself well. Organizers were always pleased with her efforts and the impact she brought to the event. It was known that Vicki and her sixth-grade class from the elementary school had taken that trip together to Washington, D.C., where they met with astronaut John Glenn and took that specially arranged tour of the White House. On that visit she was to meet the President, but he was called out of town, so instead, she had a meeting with the Vice President. Vicki had proved herself in all the special moments of opportunity offered to her, so when NASA opened a learning center in our neighboring state of West Virginia, they immediately thought of inviting Vicki, along with her sixth-grade class, to be the very first to go through the facility. Vicki was in junior high now, and her classmates from the previous year were scattered among different rooms, so the arrangements for a trip of this kind had to go through the principal. Permission was not granted for Vicki's class to attend. Instead, the principal insisted that all of the current seventh-grade class be invited to make the trip along with Vicki. If that could not take place, no one would go. Because it was important to the organizers at NASA to have Vicki be the first to dedicate the center, they gave in to the principal's demands and allowed all the students in the seventh grade to accompany her. On the day of the trip, Vicki sat on one of the buses with the students, some of whom had no interest at all in participating in this privilege and who, instead, sat and complained, saying things like, "We wouldn't have to be going to this dumb place if it wasn't for you!" Just an example of a small stab, but there were others that left deeper scars, along with many of which only Vicki knew. I can only imagine.

I must say that Vicki never complained or whined about any of this treatment. She seemed to accept all of it, maybe sponging it inside, cleaning it up, knowing that it was something she had to go through until people got it. She really didn't want to be treated any differently than all the other kids, and intuitively knew what a delicate balance she was on with them, agreeing to wait it all out. But I do remember the one time she broke down and showed us the extent of her frustration. It was the last game of the football season when Vicki finally decided to give being in a crowd a try. She opened herself to allowing the possibility of having a night of fun going to the game with her friends. The stadium was within walking distance of our home, and she was excited to be doing something so 'normal'. She was especially happy to wear her new blue jean jacket with a picture of *The Looney Tunes* embroidered on the back. She had just purchased it with money she had earned from giving a speech in Canada at an international children's festival. We stopped at a large mall on the way home from that trip and let her use a portion of the money to make a purchase of her own choosing. After all, she had earned the money. If Vicki ever got paid for an appearance or a talk, the money was put toward what we were spending to rent the plane for practice time. We had already invested much of her college savings to finance her trips, and contrary to what some others may have thought, we had never 'made money' from any of Vicki's experiences.

Vicki happily donned the jacket and left with her friends for the game. Later, as Jim and I watched television in the living room, Vicki burst through the door, crying, as she ripped off her jacket. In a mixture of anger and hurt, tears streaming down her face, she spouted, "I thought they'd get over it by now! While we were watching the game, they threw eggs at me. Some of them even hit my friends!" Then she rushed from the room. I held up the jacket that now had hardened splattered egg stuck onto its back. My heart broke. Vicki never wore the jacket again.

Okay, I guess my mother is trying to be nice. The only way to say it is that there were a number of people in my experience there who were bullying me. Hey, I've got to call it like it is: Kids and adults can do it. Which came first—the chicken or the egg? There are lots of ways to bully. Really think about that.

People there are becoming more sensitive to thoughts. That's how we communicate here. When you are there, you transfer your thoughts through speaking and writing and artistic expression, of course. But thoughts are also transmitted to others without words because they are things—a form of energy—and they can be felt. Now, if the receiver of a thought has a lot going on in his head he might get the transmission muddled up, but if the person is extra sensitive and feels how this communication works, they can get everything the sender is thinking, both positive and negative. Someday everyone will communicate like this, when you are all on the same page, and that will be cool.

I'm not blaming anyone for anything. You know, we always

have our own choices to make on what we think, say and do. I'm not saying that I was 'perfect' in every instance while I was there—whatever that is anyway. After all, we are human while we're there, and that's the challenge. What I am saying is that you people on earth can step up the game if you really become aware of the things you think and how you treat each other with your thoughts, as well as your words and actions, because every bit of it matters. There is a lot of creation going on there in your thoughts—that's where everything starts; YOU are a creator! Are you awake? Are you awake yet?

Perhaps Vicki endured these hurts without much complaint because she knew she would be leaving to go on the World Flight. These kinds of challenges would be left behind and, once again, she could go back to experiencing the best in herself and in humankind, as she did on both her previous flights. She had given her best to the world, but in her present circumstances, it didn't feel like it was being returned to her. Through it all, she remained hopeful and tried to fit into a 'normal' life in every way she knew how. That's my take on it, at least. Vicki was so deliberate in how she wanted to handle the conflict coming her way. She insisted that we not interfere. We, too, remained hopeful, knowing that the World Flight would be coming soon. That was our reasoning for limiting our involvement at school with anything concerning Vicki. We were following Vicki's lead and looking to the future, knowing that she would not have to endure overcoming the obstacles facing her at school much longer. Soon she would be on to much bigger things.

As outside speaking engagements continued and the prospect of the World Flight loomed in Vicki's future, details of Vicki's appearance took our attention. She was in those early teenage years, and she struggled a bit with choices in regards to presenting herself, at least *we* thought she did. Elizabeth was away at school and Vicki didn't have an 'advisor' for things like hair and makeup and clothes. Perhaps she would like some outside advice in these matters.

So Jim and I decided—and foolishly, I might add—to enroll Vicki in a modeling school held on Saturdays in Pittsburgh, an hour and a half away from our town. In classes, Vicki would learn the basics of clothing style, makeup, hair and all things feminine. Surely we thought, this would be of benefit to her, as we never knew what adventure was around the corner in her interesting life. There had even been mention of a cosmetics company interested in possibly helping to fund the World Flight.

Saturday classes began, and for the first one, she cooperated, but as each Saturday came, things became more and more difficult for all of us, and before long Vicki managed to make each Saturday morning more miserable than the one before it. It was like pulling teeth to get her out of bed for her to take advantage of this opportunity! On the trips there, she was ruthlessly disagreeable and made us pay for this egregious offense to her sensibilities. I can only imagine what she was like in the class!

All she allowed us to do was to drop her off and pick her up. She wouldn't abide us having any involvement in any of the proceedings. Perhaps they had a final runway show. We never knew because we weren't invited to it!

You know, sometimes you think you are doing something to help your child, and it just doesn't work out that way. Honestly, I can say that I don't remember anything redeeming about that situation except that Jim and I did purchase our first family computer while waiting for her to complete one of those mysterious Saturday classes.

Now, that was a joke! I hated every minute of it. I can see now

that you guys thought it would help me, but come on. All the time and energy people spend on how they look, how they walk—it's all pretty meaningless, and I guess I knew that. Actually, I thought it would be great if the whole hair thing was gone and everyone could be bald and just be finished with all the fussing. I knew the right clothes for me were the comfortable ones. So it just didn't click with me, and I let you know it! I guess I could have been nicer about it. You know, indulged you a bit, until you got it!

Judging ... why do you think any body or any thing is any better than any other? Where did that come from? Probably from someone who wanted some attention or power. So much time is wasted there with that human ego thing. I can honestly say I saw through that one pretty fast. Everything is beautiful in its own way. That song is right! I used to watch American Idol too, but really now. THE BEST of anything is just a judgment.

Okay, it's like this: you're down there in a 'real' world that isn't real. It's what you can't see that really counts, so why get stuck on how someone looks? It really is what's inside them that counts. And what's inside? Energy. That's the part that's real, and you have to feel it, not see it. You feel that in your heart space, the place we are all joined together as ONE. Of course some people can see it, too, but that's another discussion. Remember the Star Wars movie—my favorite of all time—that scene with everyone in the bar looking all strange because they came from different places, different worlds, different dimensions? Okay, take off the bodies ... surprise! It's love! We are our Creator's love energy trying to get out and radiate! It's the same for anyone who looks different, sounds different, acts different than you in your world on the Earth plane.

The fact is, we are all weird on the outside; you all look rather 'strange and interesting' from up here, you know. I mean, seriously, have you ever noticed how odd you all look? Just concentrate on your arm for a little while. You're a mass of 'stuffed' skin with things sticking out all over you—all of you! You all look the same! What's normal anyway? All of it, I tell you! So, please, stop it with the judgments already! I'm just sayin'. Love isn't something you do there, it's something you are, so be it, for real! Wow, I had a lot to say on that!

After the egg-throwing incident, something positive happened to Vicki. She received a letter of support from one of Elizabeth's unique and wonderful friends at her arts school. He happened to be gay when being gay was even more of a difficult road to walk than it is today. We have kept the letter, and its love still pours out every time I have had the occasion to reread it throughout the years: compassion and understanding, traveling through time and space in a written letter.

My Dearest Vicki,

Helloo, Hammy! The gift of fame and fortune (and irresistible beauty in <u>our</u> cases) <u>does</u> have its price as I'm sure you've noticed. These pathetic dorks that surround us on a daily basis soon become jealous of our gifts and try to degrade them. <u>Eggs</u>!? They threw <u>eggs</u> at you? These witless twits best watch their step. I would <u>hate</u> to think that I would have to boom up to the next football game and hurt them! Honey, I'll slip into my highest heels, my hottest dress, casually walk into that stadium and toss <u>live starving chickens</u> at the inhuman louses!

I learned, the hard way, to hold my head high when those less fabulous as myself tried to shun me. You do the same, girlfriend! You are special. Don't ever, <u>ever</u> give up hope. There are several people who know just how smart, good-hearted, and <u>divine</u> you really are! Heck, do you know how many thousands of people think you are the <u>coolest</u> thing since the ice age and don't even <u>know</u> you!? Keep faith.

Nevertheless, I must go now and sparkle somewhere else. If you have any more confrontations, give sis' a ring and I'll kill the filthy rats of moral decay! Come see us soon!

      Thinking of you, <u>always</u>!
      DMG

I recently had the opportunity to spend time with this lovely human being, and I let him know just how much his act of kindness meant to Vicki at such a tender time in her life. He holds a very special place in the heart of our family. He, too, experienced bullying for being different. The truth is, we are all different—unique in a special way all our own—so should it not follow that it's normal to be different? It's the judgment thing again, isn't it? So much unnecessary hurt because of it.

You know, it's within our power to stop this madness, but we all have to agree on it. Until then, prejudice of all kinds will remain. I guess the lesson is that we can't let anything stop us, no matter who we are, from being who we are! And, I am happy to say, nothing stopped our friend from being who he was and still is: a wonderfully kind spirit and a fabulous entertainer, sharing his light, performing for audiences in New York City to the delight of so many. His words were a gift to Vicki, and perhaps they can reach out to help you and many others who walk the path of being recognized as 'outstanding' in some way. I am honored to share a small portion of his wisdom, leaving more details and the most colorful parts to the imagination. Thank you, DMG, you are just as beautiful on the outside as you are in your heart.

I do have something to say about this gender issue: People,

you are so—here's that word again—judgmental! You can be so cruel. Hey, maybe the person you are being judgmental of is just exploring his/her energies, trying to balance them, get them working together. And the deal is, you have no idea where that other person has been before in time—what the 'who they are inside of that body' has or hasn't experienced, or what they are working on in this life.

The truth of the matter is, every human being is both masculine and feminine, together. Humans have it all wrong to think they are separate. It's pretty obvious, you know—the yin and the yang. You do have two parts to your brain, and it takes both parts working together to be a brain. Males don't carry one part and females another. All humans have both parts of a brain! The problem is, humans keep thinking instead of loving and embracing the 'who' that they really are.

Again, you guys are energy inside the body you wear. It's just a body, but may I add, you should pay attention to your vehicle, to keep it working as long as possible. It is up to you to get rid of what's blocking the flow of your loving energy out into the world while you're there; that's your business there on earth.

Eventually the body goes away, and that love energy inside of it stays. And I've got news for you: it isn't masculine or feminine—it just IS! No gender! Inside you, there is no gender! Come on, what's not to love about that!

Here's another thing to think about: if the energy that is you has been around in timelessness and spacelessness, that means it has always been. And it's been anywhere and everywhere, in all the universes in all time! YOU have probably been everything before yourself. Man, woman, sexless being -- who knows!

The creative life force is in every one of you, filling you and everyone you see with unlimited potential, each and every one of you there. What the heck, it's what's inside, remember? Just open up to feel it through your heart space! Your choice.

Could mankind be working toward some kind of super enlightenment, uniting the masculine and feminine on earth, the yin and the yang coming together? Hmmm. I have an answer to that one, but you'll have to figure it out for yourself. Now don't think too hard! If you'd just pay more attention to the energy inside your bodies, there wouldn't be so many problems there.

So much time and energy is wasted on the gender confusion issue. None of what you think is so important, matters. It's all pretty ridiculous from up here, and it's sad, too, because it's so easy to correct with a little understanding. Well, actually, it is all a game anyway, isn't it? Can you give each other a break and let everyone play in the game? We're all related; we're one! The sooner all of you get that there, the better for you and us, the ones you can't see. Maybe then you'd respect each other and appreciate all of our parts. After all, you'll join us someday, and you'll kick yourself for not having gotten it while you were there ... well, sort of ... no kicking here! ☺

Vicki was honored to have been asked to have her bio and picture included in a historical Smithsonian book about women pilots. The author and photographer came to our home and spent time interviewing and photographing Vicki. Those pictures will remain as some of the finest representatives of who Vicki was, and for that matter, still is, for in them you can feel Vicki's strength, the power of her soul. They capture the essence of her spirit. She looks ageless and timeless in them.

The photographer—who has remained a family friend through the years—had a way with Vicki. She made a real connection with her and was able to get her to talk candidly about herself, something that wasn't easy for her to do. She recorded the interview sessions, and they were included in her book, verbatim, along with all the beautiful pictures of each woman pilot who was profiled.

In one of the interview sessions, which was held at the same time that Vicki was trying to adjust to the challenges at her new school, she expressed a little of how she was feeling: "I'm twelve. So, you sort of branch off when you get into junior high. So I think the relationships are changing because of that. It's hard to tell if it's because of what I did or if it's junior high. They, like—you know—they treat me different and everything. It's starting to get back to normal, but every day someone still says something about me. I never know when to take people seriously, because they're like, "Oh, can I have your autograph?" But they're really teasing me and stuff. And they don't say nice things about me. I mean, there are rumors going around at school that I'm really this big jerk. So I don't know. It's different."

Here was Vicki speaking out to younger kids about having goals, following dreams, encouraging others in a big way about valuing themselves and their abilities and not buckling into the pressures that other people will put on them, and in her school, when she went back to her home place, this is what she was facing. Bullying comes in many forms: constant teasing, harassing, yelling out to embarrass someone, name-calling, physical assaults, gossiping, unkind words, unkind thoughts. I am not saying that everyone treated her this way, but enough did for her to allude to it in an interview for a book. Vicki so easily picked up on other people's thoughts. You didn't even have to say the words; she had a way of reading you. Something tells me she was picking up on all the negative thoughts, feeling them deep down within herself.

Wouldn't you all be so darned surprised to know that even your thoughts can be felt by other people living there? It's like this: your thoughts are things; forms, and once you think them, they are out there. Like I said before: someday that's how you will all communicate, when you're ready for it. That will take some time, and lots of evolving. There we go again with that time thing!

Your words count, your actions count, even your thoughts count. Yes, you know, those thoughts are where everything starts. Think about that one! If you could see all the garbage down there you are living in—all those sooty thoughts floating all over the place—you'd be shocked! You're living there with it. You can't see it, but it's there, swimming all around you. Now, that mind of yours can do all kinds of things. It can latch on to one of those thoughts pretty darned fast—like a pig in a slop! HaHa! Trouble is, not all of those thoughts will lead you to where you necessarily want to go ... or do they?

I remember coming home from the store to see the familiar car of a local reporter, who became a friend, parked in the driveway of our home. Splashed all over the news recently was hype about another little girl's flight from California to Florida, and I thought that he was there to share something about it with me. I saw the story covered in the media and wondered about it. The 7-year-old girl was so cute, but she was tiny, so young, so inexperienced. I knew how much Vicki had trained, completing ground school twice, passing her private pilot ground school test, completing numerous short cross-country trips and one long one, performing in an air show, practicing her flying in various weather and landing conditions, amassing not quite 100 hours of flying time in the air—all this before ever attempting her trip across the United States. I also knew that Vicki, at 11, was tall for her age, but she was not tall enough to reach the pedals of the airplane until right before the first trip. Up until that point, she had to wear a pair of her sister's shoes over her own. I knew, too, that we had not planned the national media response to Vicki's trip across the United States. It was not contrived; it just happened.

Something seemed not right here. I walked inside, groceries in hand, fully expecting to hear more publicity about this sweet little girl and her father's questionable venture into notoriety. But the news was not good. The little girl, who was supposedly piloting the small plane at the time, her instructor, and her father had died in a crash shortly after take-off in adverse weather conditions. The plane, laden with cameras, was on its way to meet the press at a scheduled event. It was tragic.

I truly do not know what Vicki felt as a result of this. I know it changed her life. I cannot know how it touched her, if she carried any responsibility for its happening, which she shouldn't have. I hope she did not. She never spoke of such things to me, to my recollection. She was immediately approached by the media for a reaction, and I must say, to her credit, the principal of the junior high kept the reporters away while Vicki was at her school, but Jim and I agreed to allow her to do only one interview, and that took place via satellite hookup from our home the next morning. She handled herself on national television with such grace and dignity. I couldn't have been more proud of her. She supported the little girl and her dreams, saying nothing negative, nothing critical. She seemed to have a higher understanding of it all, one that didn't need to be shared out loud. It was shortly after this event that Congress got involved by passing some kind of law to keep kids from flying, not that they were ever allowed to fly without an instructor anyway. How could any company financially support a trip like Vicki's World Flight now?

I remember a really great interview Vicki gave on a kid-cool television station. She was so natural, so honest, so open while letting people in on her life at home and in the air. Realizing now what she was going through at the same time in school, the poise with which she presented herself was quite astounding. She expertly handled the opportunity to reach out to young people as a role model, even though she never really thought of herself as one. She was just being real. The interview shows her at home explaining that she's just an ordinary kid who enjoys doing ordinary things. It also shows her in the cockpit, flying along with her instructor. Her competence is obvious and when asked at the end of the interview what was next for her, she brightly and skillfully replies, "What's next for me? Well, maybe I'll fly around the world, and if I do, it will be for kids everywhere. We'll just have to see what happens!" It wasn't long after that interview, the tragedy with the little girl took place. Plans immediately changed, and the World Flight never got the chance to happen. I guess there was another similarity to Amelia—something catastrophic ended her world flight, as well.

The flight around the world got cancelled because of the adult ego thing—a very sad story. It certainly served to change the course of my life for the 'time' I was there. It did lead me in the direction of other choices. What happens to one of you changes things for everyone, like dominoes falling, and it doesn't have to be for the 'worse' either. When something uplifting happens, it can change everything, too. But the way we see these happenings are judgments made in the moment. Perhaps they fit just perfectly into our picture when we get the opportunity to see that picture from a higher place. We're each on our own timeline weaving our own story, but still connected. Hey, maybe I'm doing that World Flight now!

When I try to picture what it must have been like for Vicki after that disappointment, and what it now meant for her in her everyday life, I see it like this: Maybe for her, it felt as if she were swimming, seeing a dock in the distance, with someone standing on that dock holding out a life-preserver. She knew that she had the strength to go the distance to grab it, even though she could feel all the swells that threatened to pull her under. But they weren't as important as reaching the goal. She just allowed herself to keep on swimming, knowing that she would eventually reach the dock, touch the preserver and then be pulled to safety. That knowing gave her the power to keep going. But now, the hand was no longer extended, the preserver was gone, and the dock seemed so far away. There was nothing else to do but turn her attention to combating the high waves that surrounded her, and she quickly learned that in order to survive, she had to forget about the other goals, just let go and dissolve into the choppy waters around her, letting them take her under sometimes. And so she began a new kind of journey. Vicki made the mental adjustment, and she tried to prove she was just like everyone else. And we were trying to figure out how to help her. We were all doing the best we could at the time.

Vicki's trip was prevented from taking place because of a tragic accident, or so it seemed. Could it also, somehow, in some way that we cannot know, be part of a higher purpose that is linked to Vicki? I don't know, maybe the world wasn't ready for what Vicki was planning to do. How many others received an effect in their lives by this accident happening, by Vicki not making that trip? If only we could see the tapestry of it all.

__Maybe that was the plan all along. You know, there is a reason for everything. Maybe you can't see the tapestry, but can you trust that it's there.__

As the school year ended, Vicki's need for change shouted out to us. The cancellation of the World Flight had knocked us for a loop. We had to regroup and do what was not only best for Vicki, but for the entire family. We had two other children who needed us in their lives, and we had to take some care of ourselves. I was doing some major adjustment after two years of non-stop traveling with Vicki for various reasons, topped off with my mother's health issue and my responsibilities to her. Jim's sales job required his attention, and he had been juggling everything so well, but there is a limit. The whole family had a balancing act going on. Having been caught off-guard with the cancellation of the World Flight, we were unprepared to enroll Vicki in a different school for the start of the next school year. Besides, there were no other local schools available for her to attend. We opted instead to do our best to get by with the situation as is until Vicki was a ninth-grader. We would have more time to explore options for her during the year and have her at home with us for at least another year. We all needed to settle down together. We had been to so many places, had had so many extraordinary experiences in the previous few years, and we craved to be in our own space once more, seeking peace in the simplicity of living in our small town where we had all once thrived. We gave staying right where we were a shot, that is until we could see a better choice. So the next school year began, and Vicki was back facing it, and adjusting to adolescence.

I understand that some will be critical of our decision as parents to listen to our daughter's pleas to remain as uninvolved as possible in problems at school, but after all we had been through in Vicki's journey, seeing first-hand her confidence in decision-making and witnessing her sense of good judgment, we willingly followed her lead on this. It can be wonderful to live in a small town, but then again, every place has its drawbacks. Jealousy, envy, judgment reside everywhere. We tried to rise above it by choosing not to give it our attention. We were always that way, avoiding the 'country club' scene, not seeking to impress anybody. I guess those things were not important to us. Our children were a reflection of that attitude, and we were happy for it.

As the months passed, our family, as is the case in all families, went through its share of conflict in the home. As Vicki used to say, "We're just a normal family." When it became apparent that Vicki was dealing with hurt by reacting with some hostility at home, we sought some family counseling. Growing pains in everyone's family are to be expected. We had our share of them, and my husband, Jim, found himself being the target much of the time within our family's dance, earned or not. To his credit, today, he would readily take some blame onto himself for where he was in his understanding back then. But wouldn't we all do things a bit differently if we had to do it over again? Now we each see a higher truth to the challenges that our relationships offered to us, and it's okay.

For Vicki, despite the 'help' she received, she always seemed to choose her own strategies in dealing with issues. She was detached, taking it all in stride with a no-fear way of looking at life, along with that push-the-envelope attitude. She continued to display this aspect of herself in many ways at many junctures throughout her time here. Although it was not always easy dealing with it, I had to remind myself that she could never have done the flying, made the mark that she did, had she not possessed this nature.

Pushing the envelope may seem a bit scary to some of you—lots of you—but it forces you to change things, and change is a good thing, or it can be good. Wait, that's a judgment. No judging! You've got to move forward, and pushing yourself to do some scary things sure makes that happen. It's like going through a tunnel that opens up into a paradise on the other side. Experience the tunnel—experience the paradise! It's either love or fear, people. Living in fear is not living. I came to that conclusion early. Maybe I was born knowing it.

Here's a letter to Jim from Vicki, written at the end of the first year of junior high school . . .

Dad,

I just wanted to say thanks for everything! You have been a great Dad and put up with a lot. You are always there for me. There were a couple incidents recently which I appreciated tremendously. One of them was when I wasn't feeling so good and Corinne (*that's how Vicki referred to me when she spoke with her father*) made me go to school. But instead you took me to your office and then we went to split a cinnamon bun. And while we were there we looked over the newspaper together. The other incident was similar. It was when they were checking book bags at school and I didn't want to stand there in front of everybody knowing someone would make fun of me. You understood me and we went to go split a cinnamon bun; and then you took me back to school after everybody had left. Thank you for being understanding and being there for me. You are a great Dad!!

Love,
Vicki

And Dad, I wouldn't change you one bit—and that goes for all of you in my family! You were all doing your best. Look, even in the same family there are different perspectives on the happenings of the group. Everybody's getting something different from it—having a unique experience. That's the way it's supposed to be!

Imagine all the perspectives of all the people occupying this earth space. Whoa! Talk about a big family and growing pains! Seems like the only way we can resolve all this family tension is to each go into that place inside where, despite any differences, everybody knows the ONE who is. I'm there, and so is everyone else who has walked the earth plane. We're right next to you, only in another dimension, but you can feel us when you open your heart space. What if people did just that all at the same time. Wow! Talk about heaven on earth!! ☺

There were some special people at the junior high who took an interest in Vicki and had an understanding of what she was going through—one teacher in particular. I shall call him Mr. C: C for compassion. He closely observed Vicki, and I believe he saw the light in her and honored who she was.

Mr. C was a very talented artist as well as an outstanding classroom teacher, empathizing with Vicki because he faced some prejudice himself due to his own accomplishments. Mr. C offered Vicki an opportunity to collaborate on a project with him, and she found some happiness within that recognition. He worked with her after school and sometimes came to our home. He even took the time to take Vicki on some roller-blading excursions at a popular local spot. We knew he was doing all this to boost her self-esteem, for he had recognized that need in her and had not been afraid to step forward to help. He also opened up to see who Vicki was and what the gifts she was giving meant to the world. We continue to be grateful to him for graciously sharing his kindness with her. A teacher teaching from the heart—a priceless gift.

I recently discovered—or was led to—a journal I kept on Vicki during this time, and I am astounded as I reread its pages. Vicki was speaking in public, but still trying to find her voice in the new school community where she now found herself, and I had the privilege of being her mother through it all. A peek into our lives:

October 10, 1995

One of those rare days when I felt close, wanted, by my 13-

year-old daughter. She included me in her day—told me about her protest over the superintendent's decision that the students cannot use their book bags. She asked and expected me to get her dinner—vegetarian of course. Shared that she was ready to go upstairs. Included me in on her day—the little things. I look at her and see her uniqueness—her beauty not masked by harsh words or angry thoughts. She is tall, well-formed, long legs, very pretty. I notice the cross she has begun to wear and feel warm inside to know that she is developing her personal relationship with God. As I rub her back, I remind myself of how precious these moments of sharing are.

October 11, 1995

I am reminded that it is very important for me to get across to Vicki that she must rise to her potential—even under her situation with the kids at school. They will not change their attitudes even if she remains in a "shell" to try to please them. Their opinions will remain if she is a leader or absent. Vicki needs to realize this. It is my challenge to get this point across. God help me? Give me the right words at the right moments.

I am reminded of all the personal turmoil Vicki has been through, and consequently, we've been through since her 'flights'. For the most part I've accepted the events in her life as good, but in the recent past, with her emotional reactions, I've had my moments of doubt about whether it has all been good for her to have ever flown. But I am brought back to the strong feeling in my soul's reason that Vicki learned to fly for a higher purpose—one that only the years will reveal to the world. She laughs at me when I approach that kind of subject—now.

I need to remind myself to step back and look at us both from a distance. I am helping my daughter—all my children, to reach their destiny in this life, one I did not create or decide for them. God did that along with them. I am merely an assistant along the way.

Within the last week, I went to the funerals of two young people who I knew—both killed in car wrecks. How heart-breaking for their mothers. How hard to stand back and realize that they—our children—are only loaned to us. My daughter has taught me about fear.

October 12, 1995

I see your zest for life! I know you. I'm your mother. My eyes were opened long ago to your adventuresome ways—to your fearlessness. And your father is in your life to help meet the unique challenges that you offer in that regard.

I respect your adamancy at being a vegetarian—one-and-a-half years at this point. Your love for life is shown to all creatures.

My daughter, I see you carving a niche for yourself in this male-dominated world—you are just the right blend of masculine and feminine. You still have no idea how beautiful and appealing you are to so many people—men and women. After all you've been through, you've remained as humble, more than anyone would ever know. Humble to your bones. What is life grooming you for?

October 18, 1995

I'm pleased with your maturity in taking things in stride. You don't let mistakes that you've made make you 'sick'. You told me about a girl in your class who cried because she was late and got a detention. You couldn't believe it or understand her attitude. She wouldn't face her punishment. She cried about it and got the teacher to excuse her if she brought in an excuse. That didn't seem right to you. You've got a really good head on your shoulders!

October 24, 1995

(While being a page at the State Capital) As you were in the helicopter simulators and going for your helicopter ride, which you thought was really cool and challenging, I was walking along the river that runs through the downtown, wondering what it is that life is preparing you for. I was struck by the history in the buildings, in the feeling of time through the statues dedicated to outstanding citizens. I thought about the opportunities that have been extended to you in this life, and I know they are but a preparation for something—something that will impact a lot of people. Sometimes I connect with that thought and I shiver and I have an awesomely profound feeling inside.

It all came together, didn't it? Again, there is no time, people. You have this thing called time there where you think you have to do whatever you have to do quickly. You are in a rush and miss so much. You know, if you'd just relax and look around, you'd see a bigger picture. If you did that, man, would things change there. So time is so important to you, and it is time that you need to take to see what's important. Hmm ... interesting.

Vicki spoke in the IMAX Theater at Cape Kennedy, and I accompanied her on this most special of trips where she addressed two groups of attendees at NASA's Take Our Daughters to Work Day. As usual, Vicki didn't want to advertise what she was doing at her school, so she insisted that we not share this information with them, and asked that we instead write her out as ill for the few days she would be missing. It was just easier that way. Vicki carried herself with such poise in her presentation, and once again delivered a motivational speech to the groups despite the fact that the event took place a mere week after the little girl, her father and flight instructor were killed in that terrible crash. Vicki acknowledged that it was appropriate for everyone to be there at NASA on that day because "NASA itself is no stranger to tragedy, either." She said she believed that "all the brave people who have lost their lives would appreciate us carrying on in their memory." We have a picture of Vicki in front of one of the retired space shuttles taken by a newspaper photographer who, being impressed with Vicki, sent her some awesome pictures he snapped of a shuttle take-off. Vicki kept the framed pictures in her room along with so many special gifts she received as a result of the events in which she participated.

It was on that trip that Vicki and I were privileged to take what is called a Gold Tour of the actual launching pad of a space shuttle. The tour is reserved for high-ranking governmental officials, and it was an honor to be included within this company. There was a 'bird on the pad' at the time, one being prepared for an upcoming shuttle take-off, and we saw parts of the entire space shuttle program that not many ever get the chance to see, except for brief moments on television. The experience was incredible, as well as educational.

Back home at the junior high, it seems that Mr. C, Vicki's friend, shared with Vicki's science teacher where she was in her absence. Now, Mr. S, for science, at one time also had in his class both of Vicki's older siblings, and there was a history of some—I don't know how to put it into words—adult abuse of power behaviors shown to both of them. None needs explanation now, but it all became a backdrop for the mistreatment that was now aimed at Vicki. I would guess these kinds of things are more common than we like to think. You recognize it when it happens to you. I share this not to expose the teacher, who hopefully has grown to a place of higher understanding, but to illustrate how the tendrils of negative behaviors of adults can become so destructive to a developing spirit.

Vicki eventually returned home from her trip and went back to school. What happened in Mr. S's science class isn't exactly clear to me right now, but I do know that the outcome was that Vicki missed a pop-quiz that she was not allowed to make up, and somehow she got detention because of it. Despite his knowing full-well that Vicki had just faced a very delicate moment during her absence and also that she had experienced some things that could have potentially benefited the entire class, Mr. S never inquired about her trip at all. He never spoke with her about it. He never asked her anything. He only punished her in the way he could. And Vicki accepted it.

Yes. Here we go again. You'd think adults would know better. Please, young people, don't turn into them so fast! It happens all too quickly when you give your own power of knowing away to them. Hey, I'll let you in on a secret: You kids know more about a lot of things than they do—really important truths from the other side! It's all a lot simpler than they've made it. I guess if we are really going to change things, you all have to stick it out together and use your inner wisdom—your 'little kid' wisdom—and show those adults a better way to live. I know ... when pigs fly! But you know, they really can fly, if you all think they can, and that's the truth!

And it was Stan to the rescue once again. He was an awesome reminder to Vicki that there was more adventure out there to be had, and he always made it happen for her. When he came to town to visit, he'd let her drive the Corvette and have some outside-the-box, pushing-the-envelope kind of fun. She'd get a kick out of driving around, incognito, on the highway and into some of the 'fancy' parts of town for some innocent fun. For the time, it fed the daring part of her nature. I think of Stan and what his early life must have been like; he, too, must have faced his own kinds of prejudice. He was small in stature and had a harelip, which caused him to have a bit of a speech impediment.

McGyver-like Stan was one of the most interesting,

courageous, compassionate people I've ever known. He was a Sunday school teacher who rode a motorcycle, a mentor, a risk-taker, a hard worker, an all-around fun guy to be with, and he was generous in so many ways. He really was an angel; still is (literally) I guess, and he was always up for adventure. Shortly before he unexpectedly left this earth following a heart attack, he and Jim took an impromptu trip to Costa Rica, where they rode horseback on the beach, sat in bubbly hot volcanic pools under a spewing volcano, and dug a van out of the mud on a soupy jungle road. Stan recognized a kindred spirit in Vicki, and he extended love and understanding to support her on her unique journey by encouraging her rebel spirit in positive ways. He introduced her to sky-diving, as I mentioned before, which was to eventually become her favorite flying activity. At one time it was Vicki's dream to open her own sky-diving school, and that was more concerning to us than all the flying she had done in her youth! She just loved moving fast through the air, and so did Stan.

Master: A revered teacher. You can't tell a master by how he or she looks.

A close family friend who had been witness to Vicki's vitality all her life, as both his and our children grew up together, was also a teacher at the junior high school. He came to us with a concern about her, saying, " I see Vicki walking in the halls, and I can see the light go out of her eyes a little more each day. You've got to get her out of here!" And we tried. We researched alternative places for her to go, but each one seemed to involve drastic logistical changes for our family. First of all, she didn't want to leave her brother with whom she had always been close. There was a sense of security about having him still be part of her daily life. She had already had to adjust to her sister leaving to go away to school.

Although Vicki was challenged at school, and not in a positive way, Jim and I felt that for the time being, she needed to remain in our family setting. I didn't want to push her away, but I also knew that everything would change for Vicki when Daniel graduated from high school and moved on in his life choices. No one will ever know the effect that Vicki's notoriety had on her brother in our small town. It is his story and shall remain as such, but let me say that he, too, experienced the uglier side of humanity through it. I was not opposed to Vicki continuing her education somewhere else, but I was reluctant to give up the preciousness of keeping her with us until at least the ninth grade. My thinking was that she would then be older and better equipped to handle being away from her family. True, I was a trained teacher, but home schooling was just beginning to emerge as an alternative to traditional school. If I had it to do all over again, I would choose to school Vicki at home, creating further opportunities for her to learn. The trip around the world was to be a giant leaning experience, but we know what happened to that opportunity. We were between a rock and a hard place, and time was ticking away. We continued to search out schools in other states, trying to find a fit while damage continued to happen in the days, weeks and months that passed. Vicki began changing into what she saw those around her wanted her to be. She had fought it all valiantly, but to gain acceptance, to really fit in, she began conforming, trying to prove she was just like everyone else. We knew we needed to get her out of that situation, but the longer she stayed in it the more reluctant she was to leave, and the poorer her choices appeared to be.

Look, I wasn't a 'perfect' person, that's for sure, but for a while, when I was flying, that's what it might have looked like to everyone. Well, that might have been what some people chose to believe. What's 'perfect' anyway? Look, that's why you are on that place called earth—to expand, to grow, to learn and figure out what perfect really means. Nobody is 'perfect'; they can't be. Hey, wait, or are they 'perfect' just the way they are? I just wanted to explore and experience being like everybody else and to be accepted for who I was, and I tried that, but some people wouldn't let it happen. Don't get me wrong, there were plenty of nice people there, but I found myself wanting to be friends with everybody.

Vicki shared some happy times after making friends with a kindred spirit who was in the class behind her. Meghan, like Vicki, pushed the envelope and broke ground by becoming the first girl in our town to play ice-hockey competitively, with the boys. She and Vicki understood each other and shared a lasting friendship. Meghan eventually went on to a private school in another state, where she continued on in her sports career. In the later years of their friendship, Vicki even persuaded her reluctant friend to take her first skydive when she was old enough to go without parental permission. Vicki wanted Meghan to feel how 'cool' it was to let go and fly through space, as weightlessly as possible, inside the pull of gravity. Vicki knew she would appreciate the rush, and perhaps she felt it would somehow impact Meghan's life, and I can't help but think it has.

There were other nice kids along the way who tried to share a closer friendship with Vicki, but it seemed to us she chose to turn to those who weren't as positive for her. It was almost like she did it deliberately, with intention. It remained a nagging question for years to come, "Could she be doing this all on purpose?" It really seemed that way.

Hey, maybe that was my new challenge! Maybe I made a choice to explore the lower vibrational frequencies to check them out; see if I could raise them. More about vibrations later. Life is learning about love in all forms. Do not fear love; if you do, it is you that you fear. How can you oppose yourself?

All of this leads me to what was probably the worst incident by far at the junior high school. I say worst, but then again, I did not live Vicki's life—I did not walk in her shoes; there was much she never told us. Isn't that how it is with all of us? Only *we* know the pain of the stabs; no one escapes without hurts in life. Anyway, in lunch class toward the end of that first year, she was joking with a girl who had a questionable reputation; Vicki always tried to be friends with everyone. Apparently, they made some kind of a 'bet', just a playful exchange of words between two people, joking around. Vicki always tried to laugh and to joke; it was second nature to her, and it became a strategy for her to relate to others. It put people at ease with her, allowing them to share a certain kind of camaraderie together. Humor does that, doesn't it? This was always a very sweet part of Vicki's charm; she could make people smile. After the summer passed and the new school year began, this girl started harassing Vicki, insisting that she owed her fifty dollars. We had no idea this was going on. The only reason we were to eventually learn about it was because of what happened next.

Jim and I were out of town checking on a possible school for Vicki for the next year, and we made arrangements for her to stay with one of her friends overnight until we returned. It was a new year, and football season had started, so Vicki and some of the other girls went to a football game. It was at the game when the incident began. The girl she had jokingly sparred with at lunch the previous year began taunting Vicki, following her and demanding her money. Vicki and her friend tried to walk home, but the wild-eyed, crazed girl followed them, continuing to rant and rave. A crowd gathered as the girl prepared to forcibly engage Vicki in a fight. The situation was very intense. Vicki tried to be calm and reasonable, but the girl was out of control. Vicki later told me, "Mom, if she (the girl) had had a knife, I know she would have stabbed me!" Thank goodness for some younger football players who scooped Vicki up by her arms and ran down the street holding her, until they reached a stranger's home where they hid out until they felt certain the crisis had passed. We arrived home the next day to find Vicki serving pizza to a couple of football players in our kitchen, and we were not pleased that she had broken a rule to refrain from bringing anyone into our home while we were gone. Understand, at the time, we had no idea what had taken place, but when we noticed the bruises on her face, the truth came out. Vicki invited those boys over for pizza because they had rescued her, and she was grateful. She, once again, attempted to spare us the details. After this trauma, we *had* to talk to the school administrators, no doubt about that.

We paid a visit to the office, and after a meeting with administration found out that the girl in question was a known drug user with serious family problems. They had been working to remove her from the school, but claimed they couldn't do it and looked to us to make that happen. It would take us, and Vicki, to press charges against her for the situation at the school to change. What was going on here? Vicki would have to put herself on the line in order for them to do something? Of course, if Vicki were to do that, she knew it would make things still worse. We finally got the message. It wasn't long after this incident that we came to a solution. There was a private girls' school near where Elizabeth was to finish her last year of college, and Vicki could at least be close to her. That's where Vicki would be for her 9th-grade year.

That one was pretty bad, wasn't it? True, she had her issues all right, and maybe this event started the dominoes falling for her, but for me, maybe if I really thought about my part in the incident—looked at it more closely—I could have seen that it was possible she, without knowing it, might have been teaching me some kind of lesson. At that time in my life I guess I was sort of fighting myself, and I didn't have to do that. That would have been a helpful thing to take from it. I didn't get that then, but maybe you will now.

That summer, we took a family trip to Ireland to visit Elizabeth, who, along with a college friend, was having a 'world experience' during their summer vacation. Daniel was away on a separate trip, so Jim, Vicki and I met Elizabeth, and our week was filled with lovely tours of the Irish countryside. Vicki was at the age when being anywhere with her parents was not a desirable activity; you know how that is. She remained aloof and independent, but still a part of the family group. Even though she kept her distance, she knew when she was playing a little game with us. We were on the Aran Islands at the mouth of Galway Bay riding bikes on the ancient-looking rock-filled isle, when she started an unspoken riding race. We jockeyed along the path, apart, but very much together. There was a rise on the road ahead, and Vicki powered past us in an impressive attempt to ascend the hill before any of us could reach it. She disappeared in the distance, and as we struggled to meet her at the crest, we noticed a line of sheep crossing the tiny road before us, and then we caught sight of Vicki to the right, lying in the grass beside the pavement, perched intact atop her bike, a figure still riding, only flattened upon the Irish green, on her side, going nowhere. And the rebellious teenager had a small smile on her face as we passed by and laughed.

Another evening we took in a wonderful Irish pub concert. The quaint cottage was filled to the brim with a friendly, cheerful, Guiness-drinking crowd, and the delight in the air spilled into every nook and cranny. The band played loudly, and the music was joyful. We left singing one particular song that was impossible to forget. The lyrics: *All God's creatures got a place in the choir. Some sing low, some sing higher. Some sing out loud from the telephone wires. Some just clap their hands, paws, anything they got now*! I do wish

I could sing the song onto this paper for you to get the full effect. Perhaps you are familiar with this popular Irish ditty. I remember doing my own teasing with Vicki as we made our way to the Cliffs of Moher while Jim was driving the car. Of course, in Ireland, the driver must drive in the left lane. I was in the front passenger seat, and I could no longer stand it! We were flying down narrow country roads, and I was sure we'd hit something or someone. I retreated to the backseat to sit with Vicki. We all got singing that bar song, except Vicki, who as a loyal teenager, would not participate in fun with adults. I couldn't resist. Vicki's hair was in short pigtails, and I started to pull them along with the music. She actually let me do it for a while.

I admit it, I had fun. We get a family, and isn't it a kicker for you to know you picked just the right one so you could learn something that you set out to learn in this life? So, quit the fight, learn and have fun doing it! Those parents of yours are showing you things all the time—how to be—how not to be! You have to figure things out for yourself, too, because they've been in the game longer and they've forgotten it's a game. Just love each other through it, and you can't help but win!

So, in Vicki's ninth grade year she lived on campus at a girl's school near her sister's college. We felt some security with this choice, knowing that Elizabeth was at least right up the street and we were a day's drive away. Vicki had initially begged us to move her to another school, but by the time we finally made it happen, her adjustment to circumstances at the junior high complicated the situation. I think deep down she knew she needed to go, but part of her wanted to stay. Toward the end she became conflicted. I guess that can happen when you've been pulled under the water enough and you start to forget how to swim, or at least get used to it. Vicki began anew, in a different setting. No one there would know her total story. Maybe eventually they would guess some of it, but now, she could relate to the rest of the class as a regular student. It became her fondest desire to have friends, to have fun, to be accepted, to be liked, and also to show everyone that she was not the perfect person she was once accused of being. She put her flying days behind her and continued to push her envelope in other ways. It was obvious to us that she became rebellious to prove a point. At first it was fun for her—rough on us—but fun for her. She was accepted by her fellow classmates alright. She was high-spirited and well-liked, and she insisted on proving that she was tough, a risk-taker, and would do whatever mischief the others were doing, and even more. She was too full of life and stretched the limits. I guess if she could handle flying an airplane at ten, it isn't surprising that this brand of living would follow her throughout her life. Perhaps some of the reason for it was as a result of what she had experienced the previous two years in junior high school. Eventually, this led her into some uncomfortable situations, and she learned still more about the 'ugliness' of the human condition. But I guess she asked to see it.

That first year was filled with friends, soft-ball games, tennis, happy times and challenging classes, which weren't a priority for Vicki, plus a purposefully messy room to get demerits. She broke rules and thought it was fun. The others did too, but not like Vicki. Her choices were always made with a flourish and boldness. It was as if she knew that in the scheme of life those kinds of rules really weren't that important.

She became part of the Mock Trial team as a freshman, an accomplishment in itself, garnering an award for her school as Best Witness at the State tournament. She also took painting classes. Vicki had an appreciation for art, and throughout her life continued to not only create it, but also collect art pieces every time she traveled somewhere new.

Her own artwork was very impressive; you could see she had talent. She enjoyed working with color and design elements. I loved her creations. Her painting started out bright and happy, but in the years to come, it became dark; still beautiful, but dark. It was as if she was painting the energy she saw.

I guess I pushed it; I got a bit carried away at that school, but could I have been trying to prove a point—to them, to myself? We are just the same, you and I. I told you I wasn't "Miss Suzie Perfect." We've had that discussion, already, haven't we? Did I choose to experience some things so I could help you now? Very interesting comment about the energy, Mother.

Vicki was now enjoying the experience of close friendships, as well as exercising some personal freedom to make her own choices in what she thought was a safe environment. Now she was introduced to a different kind of conflict game, one that had even higher stakes. It was in this new setting that she had the opportunity to experience the difference between a personal moral code and one dictated by those who desire control. She was about to learn how the 'system' works here on earth.

After Vicki lived on campus for that first year we re-arranged our lives so that I could move to a place close by the school and provide a home environment for her. We thought this new arrangement would be an improvement. I could keep an eye on her, and, we hoped she would focus on school work and settle down in other ways. I knew Vicki still needed me, even though she had a way of defining her life without me in it.

After 24 years as a stay-at-home mom, I took a job teaching at an at-risk elementary school nearby so I could stay occupied, giving her the space she seemed to thrive on, and advancing my own offerings to the world. Believe me, I was challenged.

Elizabeth graduated from college and was now in New York City pursuing her acting career, Daniel graduated from high school, and Jim remained in our family home while working at his job. We all had our hands full, as is the case in any active family. We make our best calls for the benefit of each family member, and it's a balancing act managing it all.

Vicki was now a day student, and that placed her in a whole new light within the hierarchy of the school. It was customary at the beginning of each new year for an example to be made of one of the students—a sacrificial lamb, so to speak, to illustrate the importance of following the honor code. Coincidentally, that student was usually a day student, one whose lower tuition fee was not as important financially to the school. Yes, there was an honor code, but Vicki had something else that ran deep within her: a strong moral code, a bond of trust she held with another person. Some may view that as merely the ability to keep secrets, but to Vicki, it was much more. Being trustworthy was a matter of personal integrity. Her loyalty ran deep. It was her own personal honor code. *She* could be trusted, but she found out the world couldn't be. Maybe she came to earth expecting that from other people, but that's not how it is here, is it? It seemed like she was repeatedly faced with that same realization. Maybe part of her knew we could all do better.

It was true that Vicki lived on the edge while residing on campus that first year, but so did many of the older girls with whom she was friends who lived there, too. Vicki, true to form, had quite a following with many of those older girls who had been there longer and who knew the ropes. I'm not sure from where it came, but an accusation was made against Vicki. Someone thought they saw Vicki do something she shouldn't have done, something she swore to me that she did not do. I am leaving out the details of the event that occurred, because frankly, I don't know the truth of it all; there was disagreement over the facts, and the truth of the accusation was questionable, but there was a giant inquiry surrounding Vicki; it seemed to be a witch hunt. The girls involved were first interviewed, and when no information came forward, they were sequestered and systematically interrogated in rooms apart from one another; grilled over and over again until someone, one of her friends perhaps, divulged some tidbit of information that could be used against Vicki that required her dismissal for breaking the 'honor code'. It was decided that 'day-student Vicki' was not a candidate for this esteemed environment. The feeling was mutual, especially after what happened next.

As I've shared, we lived practically on the school grounds; students could actually look out of the residential building windows and see our place, as well as take a short walk and be there. During the time that followed, Vicki, strong and realistic-minded, seemed to maintain herself at our home, but I knew she was hurting, trying to understand what happened. I looked into counseling for her, but once again, she refused to participate. I cannot stress enough the persistence with which she opposed this kind of interference within her experience. She continued to attempt her own method of dealing with her life challenges, keeping her own secrets. Maybe, to her, it was part of that moral code—personal integrity toward herself. I do not know.

Then we heard what was happening at the school, and it was even more startling. The school had an assembly of all the girls where Vicki's dismissal was used as an example to them, but they took it a step further. The girls were told that no one had permission to ever talk with Vicki or to ever see her again. They were forbidden to walk the short distance to our home for fear they would even catch sight of her. Now, as my memory serves me, some brave soul did just that and shared this information with her. The students were *forced* to shun Vicki, *forced by adults* to shun her, because they held the power to do it. They, in my estimation, abused their power, and its venom was aimed straight at us—at Vicki. Imagine, if you will, experiencing the opposite of world-wide acceptance. I guess being shunned in your own literal backyard would qualify. Bullying of a different kind, but still bullying. Her eyes became filled with disappointment, a disappointment in people.

Yeah, it was pretty obvious to me: freedom vs. oppression, expression vs. compression, true honesty vs. false honesty, spirit vs. ego. Hey, I know I pushed it to the limits, but maybe I was also pushed to mine. I know we all were. I don't hold anything gainst anyone, and besides, everything has its reasons for happening. I chose my own way. Maybe I left a mark with the people I touched while I was there, like we all do. We leave our mark, whatever it is, even if we don't know it at the time, or ever. That's not important.

Okay, so they wore me down, but I let that happen and I accept 'blame' on that one. I don't really blame them or myself. I just got the experience I needed, so that now I can come back in this way to let you know what's going on and help you see some things differently. It all fits together in a pretty remarkable way. I guess you've got to trust me on it. Trust, there are lots of faces to trust; that was one of my issues. Funny, it's another human thing.

Look, none of this nasty-looking stuff is supposed to make you feel sorry for me. I participated in it all. Go into your heart and feel it, then you'll know why I'm telling you this. And maybe, just maybe, when you see these kinds of things happening in front of you in your life there, you can choose to remind yourself to go inside and feel what's happening in your heart, and it can change everything.

When Vicki did the flying, soon after that first flight, she began receiving letters—letters from school children, from parents, from older people, from kindred spirits. It always meant something to her to receive them. She used to sit down and write responses to each one. She was so humble, and her messages were heartfelt and encouraging. We never told her what to say or what to write in those responses. She sent out many signed pictures and postcards to young and old alike, many to people who lived in the United States, as well as others living in countries around the world. Vicki continued to receive letters in the years that followed. She saved each one of them. Sometimes she did not respond to the person, but it was not because she did not want to. Sometimes she wrote letters and prepared autographed pictures, but never sent them. We have found those among her things. It wasn't because the desire was not there. She was dealing with other challenges in her life that didn't allow her to look to her past experience. I hope that those who wrote to her and did not receive responses can, perhaps, now understand why it seemed that she did not care to send one. It wasn't that at all. I cannot know exactly how she felt at the time, but I can guess. If you felt inspired to send her a letter, she kept it. She knows who you are, and rest assured, you have been a part of her life, and she is grateful. She has carried you in her heart, and you journey along with her in the heavens.

If we can't trust, we can't be the genuine article; we hold back and hide. It starts with trusting your own heart whispers. Probably one of the most important things you guys can be for each other in that world is to be a person who can be trusted, and by that I mean someone who sees and accepts someone else for who they are.

Hiding

The greatest opportunity for you in the life you are living there is what you are choosing to be in each of its moments.

Then something troubling happened outside the lantern, it's true,
It grew clouded with sadness; only a tiny light could shine through.
People's cruelty and judgment, their jealousy and fear
Had soiled the glass on the lantern; its light could no longer appear.

And so the little light hid from everyone,
And soon it knew its journey here was finished, it was done.
And when it left to shine again in places unknown,
Earth's people talked of how much more brightly it could have shown.

And so it was that Vicki disappeared into the halls of a public school in a place far from her hometown, to have still another kind of experience. It was there that she was able to escape from the outside world and wander unknown to those surrounding her who, by then, were members of their own cliques that had formed years before in their youth.

So Vicki became a loner, seeking refuge, perhaps, from the struggle that relationships had brought to her. But it looked to me like a deliberate choice. What was most important to her was having a job and performing it to the best of her ability. Building upon her love of movies, she began studying at the career center at her new high school, concentrating on television production. Vicki was quite a movie buff, and her video collection was expansive as well as wide-ranging, including classics, dramas, adventure, comedy, sci-fi and horror films.

One of her many jobs was working for the school system producing an after-school math tutoring program, as well as various filming assignments. This became her saving grace in high school. She never quite applied herself on the academic front, although academics were important to her, just not at this time in her life. She could quite easily have done very well; it just wasn't the focus for her then.

Observing people; maybe at this point in my NOW there, I was doing a lot of observing…

Vicki's high school years presented challenges for me, too. I saw her going even more inside herself, and I was at a loss as to how to change it. It bothered her to be around a lot of people at the same time. She hated going to the mall. If she got anything new, it would only happen if I brought selections of clothing that I thought she might like home for her to try on. It became frustrating to me as her mother. I used to think that it was me that she didn't want to be seen with at the mall, a typical teenage mindset. That could have been some of it, but the clothes—those things really didn't seem to be important to her either, and that's not typical. Now that I look at it all from a different perspective, if she went into a setting with a lot of people, perhaps she was able to pick up on everybody's energy, and it really affected her, and it was a choice for her to stay away. She didn't share a lot with me about how she really felt, but she could be disagreeable, and I could see that things were difficult for her. Again, she resisted any outside help to relieve her tensions, even from me, and instead chose to keep what was happening inside a secret.

She's right, I was all that. Some soot for my mother! I see I could have been more cooperative. What can I say? I was human, then; what can you expect? Better, from you, I hope. Besides, spies don't tell top secrets ….

Vicki experienced more heights in her life from birth to age 13 than most people ever have the opportunity to achieve, no matter their age. Now, she was experiencing the depths, and she began accepting it as normal for her. She'd have the highest hope for something, and it just didn't turn out to be what she thought. That went for people, as well as objects. Electrical things had a way of breaking around her. Watches never lasted long on her wrist; they would stop working soon after she got them. She ordered a camera online to record an important time in her life, and that turned out to be a disaster. Her computer needed some work done on it, and the man who was supposed to fix it dropped it on the floor right in front of her, and all the photos she had saved on it were unable to be recovered. Even the black Volkswagen Jetta, the car she dreamed of owning and looked so forward to getting, turned out to be a lemon, creating problem after problem for her as time went by. This happened all the time to her, so often, she joked about being a jinx.

I wasn't a jinx after all! It was that dang negative energy that was weighing me down all along, trying to balance me in that world. Remember, just because it's hanging around, doesn't mean you have to hold on to it, you know. Living there is kind of like being on a see-saw. Sometimes you go up and sometimes you go down, and it's fun to be either up or down, and getting there is cool, too, even though it can take your breath away and make you laugh or bump your butt and make you hurt or scare you a bit! I'll tell you where that place of peace is—it's right in the middle where nothing is 'good' or 'bad'. Those are just judgments, aren't they? Maybe I came to experience it all. Maybe you did, too. If I'd have known these things then, maybe I'd have stayed longer, but maybe I did know them and just stayed for a longer ride, bumps and all, until I learned enough.

As people let her down, Vicki turned to the unconditional love of animals to fill a void in her life. After all, it was much safer relating to innocent animals than to people. She begged me to allow her to get a dog. Knowing what she had been through in recent years and how much it would mean to her, I gave in, but only on the condition that the dog would be Vicki's responsibility. I do love dogs, but I knew that I was in a stressful situation myself with having to learn the ropes at my new job. I was returning to a teaching career after many years out of the loop. I purposely challenged myself by choosing to work with at-risk students. I was putting in early and late hours to meet the demands of the job, on top of going to school myself to renew my teaching certificate. Vicki's day involved traveling between two schools. Fortunately, we lived in close proximity to both of them. Vicki could come home to tend to the new puppy when she left one school to go to the next. It was a perfect plan, and based on it I made the decision to let it happen. So we purchased *Ozzie*, a cute little Pomeranian, and Vicki was thrilled, but it didn't take long before the demands of the little puppy overwhelmed her. I just could not step in to assist any more than I already did; my time was absorbed by my job. To make a very long and painful story short, after much soul searching, I ended up taking *Ozzie* back to the breeder. It was a very sad day for both of us. The puppy had done nothing wrong; Vicki had not lived up to the bargain. We were in a rented home where damage was continuing to occur each day, and things were beginning to escalate out of control. I had to do something about it, so despite my repeated warnings should the situation not change, Vicki continued to neglect her promise to me, and I chose to return the dog. When I finally had the courage to follow through on my warning, Vicki was so upset with me. It was pretty unforgivable in her book. To this day I still feel a twinge in my heart about it all, but I know it had to be done for everyone's sake, including *Ozzie's*, who, incidentally, had his name changed to *Fred* when he was adopted immediately by a new family with a happy little boy in it.

I guess just like I received unconditional love from an animal, I needed to show you some, too, Mother, by forgiving you then. I could have; I know now that when you forgive, you can skip lots of steps and let go of things you don't need to keep inside of yourself, and that's good. I just could have done it earlier, but how do you know I didn't? Could I have been trying to teach YOU something here? Besides, I came there to learn some lessons, too. You all do, and each soul energy serves its higher purpose for the whole of it all—the BIG ONE! Maybe that little boy needed Fred more than I did. ☺

Then, there was *Nellie*. Vicki was enamored for the longest time with ferrets. In fact, upon landing the space shuttle simulator at Johnson Space Center after her flight across America, she told a reporter, "My Dad promised to get me a ferret if I landed it, and now he has to get me one!" That story followed her on some of the television shows on which she was a guest. Nothing against ferrets, but they weren't on my personal lists of must-haves! We talked her out of a ferret because the neighbor across the street had a mansion of a house, and their ferret went missing inside it somewhere, and they never found it again.

I guess that outcome convinced Vicki to go for the offer of a beautiful Siamese kitten instead. She named her *Monique*, but *Monique* turned out to be *my* baby, so, after the *Ozzie* fiasco, how could I now refuse her request for a ferret? I knew how much animals meant to her, so somehow I found myself at the local pet store, and we walked out the door with a ferret—the last one left, as a matter of fact, and it had already been returned. That's all Vicki needed to hear; it was ours!

We purchased a big cage, ferret food and lots of toys—everything we needed. We were now in our own place, and with *Nellie* in a cage I figured things would work out this time. I can't say that Vicki didn't try with *Nellie*; she was determined to make this a successful experience. The one who didn't cooperate was *Nellie*. She turned out to be what some ferret people call a 'biter'. Vicki had to wear thick, heavy work gloves when she lifted *Nellie* from the cage to clean it.

One time during the cleaning process, *Nellie* leapt up at Vicki's face and latched on to Vicki's chin with her teeth, not letting loose her hold. In my mind's eye, I can even now see Vicki painfully walking toward me, the ferret hanging from her face! I still don't know how we got her off. My greatest fear came when I had to be a babysitter for *Nellie* when Vicki had to leave town for a number of days, and I was left with the job of feeding and caring for her. It was frightening! I did live to tell the story, though!

Later, when it was time for Vicki to go to off to college, she found a good home for her. We kept in contact with the animal lover who became *Nellie's* new mother and later learned that *Nellie* turned out to be a well-adjusted, playful and happy ferret, enjoying a very full cage-free life. She had free reign of her new home and some other animals to pal around with, and she was loved. I guess Vicki must have done something right with her; it surely wasn't me.

Hey, you never know, do you? I did love Nellie. Too bad I didn't look at what was happening with her as a message to me about where I was with relationships. Nellie was fighting me. I guess I was fighting my mother. Maybe, I was still fighting myself. Maybe I hadn't stopped. Again, some advice: look at what you think is happening TO you, then change it around and really listen because it just might be trying to tell you something. "What's this reflecting back to me?" If I had done that, maybe it would have changed some things ... or not. At least, I'd have thought more about it all! Not sure how we got Nellie unhooked from the chin either! Glad she turned out happy.

As I said, Vicki didn't like being in crowds, but I can say this—she would go to a baseball game at the drop of a hat! Or she would be up for some feasting at her favorite Mexican restaurant with her closest friend from high school who also attended the career center. It was a treat to be with Vicki and share a laugh. After Vicki left the earth, her friend and I reminisced about that blissful feeling and how special it was. Even during the most trying times in her life, Vicki could laugh a laugh from the depths of her soul, and you just felt this deep connection with her on a level you couldn't explain. Something magical always seemed to happen when she'd laugh. It didn't have to be about anything hilarious either. There was just a joyful connection with her; it was contagious. It lit up the room. It reminded me of how it was when she, Daniel, and Elizabeth were all little, growing up, loving life together.

I've told you this before: life is to be enjoyed—all of it! ☺

And no matter what happened to her, she absorbed it like a sponge. Her choice was to hold it all inside. Maybe she spoke of her feelings with someone, sometime, but I doubt she shared all of it. Vicki's life so far had shown her countless experiences within many different settings in a few short years. I think it gradually became obvious to her that she *was* in some way very different from the people who surrounded her. That admission led to the choice of trying to remove herself from it all, and after teenage experimentation with alcohol, she began making a habit of softening the blows of the world by secretly drinking. It gradually became her escape from the disappointments of this life. Still, along the way she helped other people with her kind of wisdom, the kind only she could share—in smaller ways now—one on one.

Only the people who knew her in that way will understand this. I had a probing conversation with that close friend from high school as my concerns increased around her activities: what I knew, what I thought I knew, and what I didn't know. Vicki's independent nature was a giant challenge to me—to all of our family. When making decisions in regard to their children, parents walk the line between trust and vying for some kind of control—all to help their children as they grow. Each child in our care is an individual, and I always thought it was up to me as a parent to honor them by trying to understand the *who* that I knew them to be. But we do make our share of mistakes along the way. In asking questions of her friend, I attempted to gather some information by opening the curtain to peek into her world—the one she so skillfully hid from me. I asked him, "Do you think Vicki needs help of any kind?" His response to me was solid: "Vicki has her head on straighter than anyone I know. *She helps me.*" I trusted in that recognition. I hoped that the Vicki inside what I was seeing on the outside was the strong spirit that I knew in my heart was still there.

Warning! Warning! Watch out; you can get carried away with that kind of thing—escape by substance. I guess I did that, and it's part of my story. I'm responsible because it was my choice. Maybe to you it looked like a mistake. Maybe it was. Hey, we all make mistakes. Like I said before—it's a perk of being human. I'll let you in on a secret: what you call a mistake is just a different experience, a different way of being there. You came there to feel the experience you chose to have. So relax, but be aware of what you are doing; that might change your choice, you know. You can change a choice at any time. Give yourself and other people a break. Whatever ends up happening, it's not the end of the world. Interesting comment. You and a world will still exist ... somewhere!

Eventually, Vicki did graduate from high school. It came at a rough time for all of us, because my beloved mother, my treasured friend, passed away a couple of weeks prior to this milestone in Vicki's life. I say milestone, but it was all very anti-climactic for her. She had so many fabulous experiences early in her life, and I knew that her high school experience was more of a challenge than anything she had faced earlier. I was along for the bumpy ride through it all. She was accepted at a fine college where she chose to major in television production, and I looked forward to her future there. The day of her graduation we had some simple appetizers at the house before going out to a fancy dinner. It turned out to be a nice time for us all: Jim, Elizabeth, Daniel, Bob—her first flight instructor—me and Vicki. When we arrived back home, she found some lovely roses at the front door that her best friend had left while we were gone. Graduation was Vicki's last stab at demonstrating just how different she really was. She almost didn't appear on stage with the other graduates. For days before the event I asked Vicki repeatedly if there were any special instructions, any specifics on shoes, clothing, etc. She wouldn't share any written information with me, so I had to rely on her verbal remembrances and her judgment calls. Well, we got the dress right, but not so lucky with the shoes. I don't remember now whether the controversy revolved around the color of the shoes or that they be open toed or closed, but I do remember questioning her a number of times on the details. Anyway, she wore the totally wrong shoes. If it hadn't been for one of the assisting teachers who traded shoes with Vicki, we would not have seen her receive her diploma on stage with the others. Well, I guess if it didn't bother Vicki, why should it bother us? We were still proud of her, knowing full well all she had endured to get there on that stage with the others.

Come on, why should that be so darned important, anyway—the color of some shoes? Open toes, closed toes? Get real, or should I say—get a life! Well, actually, you do get one—another and another and another and—LOL! You know, you live all kinds of lives while you are there, I did. Your thoughts can create endless possibilities, not only in your NOW there, it can take you on journeys into other dimensions. There are so many of those out there. Science is just waking up to that fact. With all that going on, who cares about shoes? Give me a break!

As a graduation gift to each of our three children, we offered them the choice of a trip to a place of their choosing. One of us would go along with them. Elizabeth chose to expand her horizons on a tour of Europe, and I accompanied her on that whirlwind bus tour. Daniel made a similar choice, and this time Jim went along with him to share the adventure. I am so grateful we made each trip happen. Now, it was Vicki's turn, and since she had already been to Europe, her choice was to go on a cruise that included Norway and part of Russia, with a side trip to the Arctic Circle. I was going to go with her on that one, but with my mother's passing, I just couldn't make the trip, so, instead, Vicki and Elizabeth took it together—something that turned out to be very important for both of them. Being over seven years apart in age, they were always at different stages in their lives, and this trip offered them memorable bonding moments that would last a lifetime and longer. I am so glad that trip happened for both of them. Later, I got the chance to go on a trip with Vicki to Cancun after she graduated from college. We had the 'scuba instructor from hell' there who could actually yell at you under the water and scare the suit off you! We laughed about that every time we recalled our experience. I am so grateful I had the opportunity to spend that time with her. We stayed in a hotel that was shaped like a pyramid, with long, straight hallways leading to all the rooms on each floor. I have a picture of her somewhere along one of those corridors leading into a place that disappears in the distance behind her. She is standing in the middle of the hall, wearing white capris, a black top, carrying a package, and she is waving at me. The black and white against the mystery of the unending corridor going who-knows-where makes a dramatic scene, and she is smiling at me.

Yeah, that was cool. Glad you remember that image, Mother!

After the trip with Elizabeth, Vicki began another rocky road on her path of becoming 'educated'. I say 'educated' because I now know how full of wisdom she really was all along. Her first year at college quickly became shrouded in mystery. She began skydiving when she should have been at school, and eventually she left that college, trying to find what she was looking for in New York City with her sister for a while, and also with me in North Carolina where

I continued to teach during the school year. Eventually she began college again at still another location, but with her independent nature she made whatever she did there her business and certainly not ours. We were involved as far as she would let us be.

Vicki would finally end up back in our original hometown at our family home, going to the same university I had attended, and from which I graduated. She was a commuter and pretty much had the house to herself. Jim was still there working and preparing for retirement; I was still teaching in another state, returning on vacations and during the summer months.

Vicki was doing well in school, no doubt, but she kept her distance in her relationships with us, her parents, at least. She was closest to her brother then. She demanded the space to be whatever it was she wanted to be, and we were all challenged by her.

Yes, my relationship with my mother was different than my relationship to my father, and my relationship to my sister was different than my relationship to my brother, but we are all connected. Only we know who we are within each of those relationships, and just our side of it at that, unless we choose to look deeper to see something of ourselves there, something available for us to learn. That's why you are in that family together. Like I said before. to be in a family is no accident! Learn from each other in this space of love that you create together, trust each other, allow each person in the fam to BE who they are. If everyone did that there, things between all of you would be so much better.

You are only one point of being, one ray of the sun pointing its light in one direction, but when you make an effort to see the lights around you—aahh—that's when you join in with others and become a bigger, brighter light together. That's what my family is

doing now, and I'm still a part of it!

There was always a job in Vicki's life. We marveled at her work ethic. She unfailingly gave her best to whatever job she had and excelled in doing it. It seemed important to her to experience different and wide-ranging employment—almost like it was a challenge of some kind; she thrived on it.

Her first job was working at a food both at the county fair. She enjoyed being with people then, and the booth was next to the horse ring, another plus. After her flights she established herself as a capable and trustworthy 14-year-old, so she took a job as a night manager at a gas station along the interstate. She pumped gas and cleaned windows, deposited money, and closed up at night. We were a bit concerned over that, but Vicki had no problem with it. I remember a woman whom I did not know sharing with me at a local restaurant that Vicki had been especially kind to her when she stopped for assistance and that she never forgot it, and I guess I haven't either.

Vicki went on to work in a music store, a book store in New York City, at a number of video stores, that job behind the camera at the cable television station, and also in factories for a couple of summers. I remember one of the guys she worked with leaving a really touching message on her legacy website after she left. He talked about what a really genuine person she was—a regular human being despite the notoriety she had earned as a result of her earlier accomplishments. Vicki continued to be able to relate to whomever she was with in a real way—nothing put on; that wasn't her at all. And she would later go on to join the United States Peace Corps. She seemed certain she wanted to pursue that avenue, and as soon as she applied, she was accepted. She so wanted to help the world. Maybe it was partially because her chance to do that was cut short when the World Flight got cancelled. Maybe it was because John F.

Kennedy had always been her presidential hero, and he started the Peace Corps. I cannot be certain of her whys, but perhaps it had to do with the global way in which she viewed the world.

And then, there was the last job she would hold while on the earth. After the Peace Corps, she came home and knew she needed to find employment, so she explored some possibilities which to us seemed limiting. Her degree was in criminal justice, and Vicki insisted on taking a job that placed her in the catacombs of existence. She became an investigator of people who were suspected of insurance fraud. More on that later. The interesting thing about it all was that Vicki didn't even always cash her work checks. She never knew what was in her checking account. It was as if she was doing all this work just for the experience, not for the pay.

Yep, each one of those jobs was a learning experience. Maybe at some level I knew I only had twenty-six years, and I had to get it all in. Remember, I did tell you when I was a kid that I wouldn't live long. The money thing—I just could never get a hold of that one. Could it be because that isn't really important? We don't deal in any of that where I live now!

Some people might say that Vicki 'suffered' from a state of depression. That's the medical term for it. We sought out help for her all along, offering it to her. That took place many times throughout the years. We set her up with several counselors, but it always ended in the same way: her will to do what she wanted to do was stronger than anything; her actions were purposeful. I can see that more clearly now, but at the time it was all so confusing, perplexing and frustrating. She went to a gathering in New York City that was supposed to empower all the participants, but it had no effect on her. She attended two separate Outward Bound experiences that are also designed to be life-changing. One was a no-frills sailing adventure in the Florida Keys, the other a 14-day hiking and whitewater rafting adventure out west that included rock climbing and a solo experience. None of it got to her, at least that's how it looked to us. She completed it all, but it was almost as if she didn't want any of it to affect her, who she was being.

Well, there came a time when we got together with some family members, along with a trusted family friend, and we staged an intervention for her. It is all too complicated and unnecessary to explain what happened, but needless to say, it did not prove to be the magical solution for what we perceived as her problems, at least in the way we all thought it would. The good news was that after her refusal to cooperate with the plans we had made for her, she became much more open to her father and to me, talking more with us and sharing her feelings. She settled down and became totally focused on fulltime, year-round school.

You know, I wanted no part of that scene! Think about it—how do you know for sure it was not my choice to experience the dark you saw as 'suffering'? Were you trying to force me into doing what YOU wanted me to do based on some way YOU thought I should be? Think about that when you try to do this to someone. Maybe the person you are so concerned about is being that way because they are meaning to gain something from it in a place you can't see—do some personal work at a deeper level.

Now, that doesn't mean you don't try to help a person if you see them in a challenging time in their life, but don't assume that YOU can change what's happening. Only they can change if they choose to. Maybe that's the way they need it to be. So you've got to make your choices about things and allow other people to make theirs according to the secret place inside of them. It all fits into the plan somehow. And please don't go blaming yourself about someone else's choices. Trust.

Some of you may believe that I made wrong choices—and believe me, I am sure that's what they looked like—and if you do, that's perfectly okay with me. You are free to make your own choices, but maybe you can learn from the ones I made. Maybe that's part of why I made them. That's how it works.

Another thing: all that looking at other people's 'stuff'. Why are people so interested in prying into other people's lives all the time, assuming they know what's best for them? Believe me, there is plenty to look at in your own life. Why not choose to go deeper and look inside yourself? I'm here to tell you that's where it's at! There's a lot in there to see that can help you in the NOW. If you'd all do that in the first place, maybe nobody would be intervening with anybody; they wouldn't have to. It would all be cool.

Let me add this comment about helping yourself. I know it's rough there in that life sometimes, but when it is, do consider talking to somebody. Don't be afraid to do that. You have runners around you in your earthly life just waiting to help out, and hey, there are so many of us on the other side hanging in there with you, ready to help if you'd just ask. With all of that help, you can make your own decisions about how you want to BE there. That's what you end up doing anyway, don't you?

No matter how much you talk to someone, there are just some places no one else can go. You've got to go in there yourself. It's your work to do. I knew that, but everyone around me at the time didn't know it. That's okay.

The results of each decision you make in your life is meant for you to learn whatever it is you came to learn in the first place. YOU are the one who knows that ... even if you don't think you do. We're all in that 'vegetable' soup together!

Oh, and for those well-meaning helpers, bear in mind that 'helping' doesn't always work the way you want it to work. That doesn't mean you don't offer to try to help someone, but for your own sake, just don't get attached to the outcome. Somehow, whatever happens is okay.

Had a lot to say on that one, too!

While Vicki was immersed in school, Jim and I knew that she needed a companion. Once again, it was the animals to the rescue! On a weekend anniversary trip, Jim and I spent a good deal of our time searching out a surprise for Vicki. After reading ads in papers at breakfast one morning, we ended up somewhere in the countryside of New York at a farm where several different breeds of puppies were for sale. In a coop-like building, we walked by cages of darling little creatures, stopping in front of the one that held several baby Cairn Terriers behind the wires. A group of them charged forward to greet me, but one stayed behind. Her eyes met mine and she slowly made her way to me past all the other puppies, and it was she, *Mya*, who Vicki eventually scooped into her arms and couldn't let go when we arrived home later that evening. *Mya* slept next to Vicki each night, sharing her moments, high and low, sharing her secrets, as our precious animals willingly and loving do for us. We still have *Mya*, and there is something about her calm, magnetic, but willful nature that continues to remind us of Vicki.

It was a few years later, after a visit with Elizabeth in New York City, Vicki insisted that *Mya* have a companion. *Mya* accompanied Vicki on that visit, and Vicki observed her interacting with *Annie*, Elizabeth's Jack Russell terrier. Upon their return home, Vicki felt a sadness in *Mya*, and she began a planned, systematic 'attack' to allow still another canine to be brought into the fold. I was not for it, and playfully dodged her schemes, toying with Vicki myself by establishing that the dog had to be older and trained.

In between her school and work, Vicki researched to find just the right addition for our family. She located a little Maltese that was nine-and-a-half months old, whose training was almost complete, and the real clincher for Vicki was that he was supposedly blind in one eye. That's all Vicki needed to know. She insisted that we take a ride to see this dog. After much protest on my part, I finally agreed to a fact-finding mission.

Of course, a further agreement was made before leaving: we were not purchasing the animal that day. This was to be an exploratory mission only. Right. There were still other possibilities to investigate. Sure. Once Vicki laid eyes on the dog, it was all over.

So we left with a dog in tow, and one of us was happy as heck! His name was *Sampson*. Vicki, however, had a much different name in mind for him. On the ride home, in true Vicki style, she changed his name to *Jose*: a little Maltese named *Jose*. We laughed as we drove along, singing songs to him. My song was sung to the Star Spangled Banner— *"Jose can you see?"* Vicki's catchy, little two-note ditty was much more creative. Wish I could sing it to you here— *"His name is Jose. He had no place to play. They said he was blind, he prove them wrong, he walk a straight line."*

So, it was that *Jose* joined *Mya* on the bed next to Vicki, and all was well—at least for a little while. I'll cut to the chase: Jose's breath was horrendous, he had a temper, and left his mark everywhere, but you could never actually see him do the deed! A couple of months after getting him, Vicki finally took him for that first doctor visit and found out that he was not nine-and-a-half months old, but nine-and-a-half years old. He had to have practically all his teeth pulled because they were abscessed. He was not a young, nearly-trained puppy, making errors around the house, but a dirty-old-man dog doing whatever he liked!

Still and all, we grew to love Jose, even though he was something else. He was once put under house arrest by the 'dog police' for biting the cable guy inside our house! I made a personal promise to Vicki that I would always take care of her two 'babies', and I did so until Jose's passing a couple of years ago at age eighteen. Funny thing is, after he left us, I understood that it was Jose that had been taking care of me all along.

Duh! Yes, the dog was for you after I left so that you could move through the process of gradually letting go and knowing truth. Mother, you were the one that couldn't see! Oh, sorry, you were only half-blind. LOL! Animals: little bundles of love surrounding us when we're there, holding the space for us to feel unconditional love, taking care of us. That's pretty cool.

So began Vicki's return to achievement at college, and once again she slipped into obscurity, until one of her professors noticed. It seems the prof, who is now a family friend, put two and two together as she read the newspaper and found a familiar name in the section that recounts historical happenings of the day. One of Vicki's flight days, which had taken place nearly ten years before, was featured that day, along with her name, of course. The professor recognized that there was a student in one of her classes with the same name, and after class she questioned an embarrassed Vicki and discovered the truth. I guess that's some proof of Vicki's continued humility as she walked through her life here on earth.

She went on to manage balancing a full year-round schedule of classes along with working, and then graduated summa cum laude, with a degree in criminal justice. I'm not sure why she chose that major, although I can see the fit now, in retrospect. Perhaps her intentions were to go into law someday. She was multi-talented and certainly highly intelligent, and she could have done anything she wanted to do. She had once been toying with becoming a doctor.

She used to sit and watch those operation programs on television. It didn't bother her to see the doctors opening up different body parts. You could tell she was just observing something. I don't think she was sure herself what the future would hold. One thing I do know, she definitely wanted to join the Peace Corps.

It was nothing for Vicki to hop in her car and drive across the country by herself, and that's what she did in the months before receiving her final Peace Corps assignment. She stayed in a little place out west, one that Jim had been grooming for a retirement destination and where we would eventually move after Vicki left this world to join the next one. She loved hiking in the canyons there and being alone out in nature. She fed the hummingbirds outside the back door and left strict instructions for Jim to keep up this ritual whenever he made a trip out there after she left for her Peace Corps service.

As I have grown in my own understanding, I can now see that Vicki had a deep connection to the land, and she possessed Native American sensibilities. There is a Native American saying that goes something like this: You go to the city to find people, to the ocean to find love, to the mountains to find yourself, and to the desert to find God. Our place out west was a combination of the mountains and the desert. Perhaps Vicki found what she needed in her time there alone with the rocks and the sky and the birds.

Covering vast distances was easy for her to do in her white Jeep. After traveling back east from out west, she got right back in her car, driving first to Texas to pick up her brother on break after his first tour of duty in Iraq, then heading to Chicago for their cousin's wedding, and finally driving Daniel back to our family home for the rest of his leave.

Yes, hiking. You've got reminders all around you to let you know who you really are—the energy inside. You are your own point of light, of being, and everything and everyone you see is energy along with you. Your energy is vibrating at its own speed. Everything is vibrating—everything! The faster the vibration, the higher the frequency. The higher the frequency, the deeper connection to All That Is. A hike in nature is a great way to raise your own vibration and to feel that connection.

Speaking of raising your vibration—NOW is the time to raise the roof on yours. When you raise yours, you help to raise the vibration of all humanity. Living in the earth plane is a challenge because there are so many different frequencies going on there. The lower vibrations can threaten to pull higher frequencies down. But the good news is that high frequencies can raise the lower ones, so it is up to you to participate in making that happen—if you choose to—and we on this side of things are looking for that to happen. So, how do you do that? Change what you allow yourself to 'think'. It's as easy as you want to make it, or as difficult. The choice is yours—always yours.

I did love to hike, to feel the sky and the rocks and the trees, and to be free. You can actually hear it all speak to you—feel it lifting your vibration—if you are quiet and listen. I didn't do it enough while I was there. I wish I had. But you *can now.*

As I said, for years Vicki talked about joining the Peace Corps. Maybe it started with her admiration of John F. Kennedy, the president who began the outreach program for altruistic young people to make the world a better place. Vicki had given that charge to so many herself when she gave her speeches in years prior. She told audiences of her peers that it was up to all of them together to change the world. I believe she settled on applying to the Peace Corps when college was completed, after she interned with a private detective. She applied, was interviewed and immediately accepted.

Vicki was thrilled and couldn't wait to hear what her assignment would be. Which third-world country would be her home for two years? They all needed help that she was willing to give. I remember when the packet with the selected country came in the mail, she admitted she was disappointed at being assigned to the country of Moldova, a very small, poor, landlocked, breakaway Russian country located between Romania and Ukraine. Not much going on there except that it was known to be the second most depressed country in the world. The people drink a lot there, too; kind of goes together. That was a big concern to us. In true Vicki style, she just laughed at the irony of once again being disappointed, but she did not want to refuse her assignment and wait for another one to pop up. Perhaps she was thinking that she would go where the chips had fallen and proceed forward from there. She was ready for a new challenge anyway, and the high esteem in which she held the Peace Corps was the perfect choice for her. Maybe, she thought, finally, she would be in a situation that called for the finest, the highest and best from everyone. She could be a part of a positive influence, not only to an entire country, but to herself, as well. She was ready for bigger things. She had studied all the materials, along with the strict rules and regulations to which Peace Corps members must adhere, and she was prepared to do her personal best and to abide by them all.

Soon she was packed and on a plane headed to a major US city to have an initial meeting, and also some basic language lessons. Peace Corps people must learn the language of their country assignment and must communicate as such, right from the start. They each initially live in a small village with a family where they learn the ropes, so to speak, before they get their final work assignments within the country according to the jobs they will hold. So it was shortly after that introductory period in the United States that she was whisked away to a small village, spending her very first night in a very foreign country along with a family who spoke a different language.

We were not to learn what happened that first night until a long time later. Vicki kept it to herself until she could no longer do so. It seems the family she was staying with had invited extended family to their home for a celebration of sorts. There was drinking going on, something very common in this culture, something that would prove to be a challenge for Vicki. That night, Vicki, fresh off her long trip to this new place, retired and dressed for a much needed night's sleep, an uncle slipped into her room and crawled into bed with her. Now, only Vicki knows what truly happened after that. I do not, for she would only eventually tell me a small part of it and certainly would not admit to all that most probably happened. Imagine, a young woman dreaming only of helping to make the world a better place, arriving just that day in this new country to a home provided to her through the Peace Corps, being there for just a few short hours, and then while she tried to sleep, being taken advantage of. I can only imagine what Vicki experienced, how it made her feel. Much later, she would share with us the reason she had not spoken up sooner: "I didn't want to make an international incident." So she absorbed it, keeping it all to herself a lot longer. But it influenced her in the choices she made while living there in the months that followed. And now, the reasons for those choices are more clear to us. No one will know the full impact on her of the event that took place that night. Things like this happen to many girls, boys, women and men, and the effects linger for a lifetime.

Lots of soot here! Hey, the body, it's just a vehicle, remember? And in some cases we just have to remember that. In my life there, this was one of those times. The truth is, we are all constantly giving out 'wisdom' to each other. Could it be that in all those situations throughout my life where it looked like I was being punched down, a victim of something, could it be that I had a part in choosing to be a vehicle for the punchers to see themselves—to remember someday what they did—if and when they choose to see? It all comes out in the end. LOL! There is no end!

The animals in a third-world country are not treated with the respect that they are in more economically blessed places. I try to imagine how Vicki must have felt as she saw neglected dogs and cats wandering listlessly in the streets each day. Once, when Jim and I traveled to Moldova to visit Vicki, we stayed in a hotel in the downtown area of her city, and all night we heard the unsettling cry of wild dogs barking in the streets below. Some of her Peace Corps family recall that Vicki, on several occasions, managed to sneak a stray cat into her hotel room and care for it when they made long treks to the larger city for meetings and had to stay overnight. I also remember Vicki telling me about a little puppy she took into her home. She named him *Bear,* and seeing his picture, she made a good call on that one! She showed him love and care, and when she found someone she felt would continue to treat him with compassion she willingly gave *Bear* away to him.

Probably the most unusual animal story from Moldova revolves around a rat. Yes, a rat. Vicki purchased one in one of the larger cities and brought him home to live with her. The winters are harsh in Moldova. What makes it especially difficult there is that the electricity does not always work. It can be off for days at a time, and when it comes on it may only be for a short time. This particular winter was extremely cold, and it was well below freezing for days in Vicki's apartment where she lived by herself. She slept fully dressed in layers of clothing, along with coat, gloves, a warm hat, and with something else tucked under the layers of blankets covering her. The little rat slept there too, kept safe, alive, by Vicki's warmth—the love that flowed from her heart.

I always felt pure, unconditional love from the animals on the earth, but it's in the plants and the flowers, and the water, everything. It's all alive with love. That's the energy I've been talking about. It's all around you, and it's all you need—it's food for your soul. The love you feel gets shared when your heart space is open. I've told you before, you are love, so just admit it and be it for real! That's the only REAL thing down there. It's not Coca-Cola, it's LOVE!

During Vicki's years in Moldova we were aware that she carried the burden of concern for her brother, Daniel, who shipped out to Iraq for his second tour of duty. It wasn't as if she didn't have her own problems to worry about. But, who had the real anxiety here? The parents were the ones with two children in positions of peril, both in foreign lands at the same time! Nevertheless, we knew that her brother's well-being was always on her mind. She made her way through the maze of physical, mental, social and emotional tests that her newest endeavor brought, while enjoying the camaraderie that she and her Peace Corps friends shared as they adjusted to life together in a new country. The bonds that are formed during these moments in their lives are lasting. We were very grateful to her Peace Corps family for their loving support during Vicki's service, and to us after Vicki left the earth.

It must have been challenging for Vicki, a vegetarian for over ten years, to make the drastic change of adding meat to her diet. The butchering of chickens and rabbits in the backyard was an everyday occurrence in life where she then lived, and so was drinking. They commonly grow grapes, making their own barrels of wine that are stored right outside the kitchen door. On our visit to the country, we were treated to a long, leisurely lunch with a village family at whose open-air home Vicki once stayed. Although we did not speak a word of Romanian, and they did not speak English, we experienced the warm hospitality, the fun, and all the generously flowing and unrequested homemade wine refilling of our glasses all afternoon. What can I say? "When in Rome," turned into an evening of recovery for me! I could see how tested Vicki was each and every day. I think she wanted to experience happiness alongside the people there in Moldova. Just like the people in that country, she too yearned to be happy. Watching the movies that we sent to her from her extensive personal collection was a favorite past time: all the seasons of *Seinfeld* as well as *Absolutely Fabulous* got a lot of wear, and brought some of home to her. Any opportunity to explore areas both inside and outside of the country were always welcomed by her. I am not saying that she didn't have enjoyable moments and share happy times with people there—I know she did. I just think that it got harder for her to see her way in the depression of this atmosphere.

It was getting hard for me to see. I could have chosen differently, but, hey, I was seeking to experience life—the full spectrum of frequencies—all of it, and boy, did I, let me tell you! Wait, I can't tell you everything!

I think it didn't take Vicki long to see that even in the Peace Corps, in her mind a highly respected institution, things were not as they appeared. Throughout Vicki's life, she observed how people are unkind to each other. She experienced being treated unfairly, being taken advantage of, being bullied. It was everywhere, from kids to adults. Now, she had a chance to see it happening on an even larger scale. As she related to me some of the situations confronting her in her job, I sensed she had kind of an x-ray vision of it all: the ability to see through the superficial, right down to the truth of a matter. Vicki's job in her tenure involved grant writing. She would secure monies for a project and then expect to see them properly allocated, but that did not always happen. She felt responsible for the disbursement of the funds, but as she watched them being diverted, she realized she had no control over the situation. She was now witness to an entire country taking advantage of another, using donated resources, willingly given, but expected and taken without gratitude. That display of greediness was very hard for her to accept. I heard her disillusionment when she eventually shared a conclusion with me: "I thought I'd be going to Africa or somewhere and digging ditches, or improving the water systems—doing something meaningful and lasting." What began as a dream to make the world a better place revealed other parts of life that didn't make sense to her.

Without passing judgment on the entire program, I'd like to add this. Much is expected of these young Peace Corps volunteers who come forward with love in their hearts to do something of service for mankind. They risk their health, their lives, to make this contribution, and the safety of their living conditions while they give this gift should be ensured.

Let me digress here for a moment and talk about something seemingly unrelated to the subject at hand: Gratitude—that's a big one, on all levels. I didn't always show my gratitude on the outside, and if I had to do it all over again, which I can if I want to (you probably won't understand that, and it's okay) I'd have expressed it more while I was there. But gratitude is a lot deeper than just saying thank you to someone for doing something nice for you. Can you have gratitude for everything that happens to you in your life? If you did that, it means you'd have to accept everything as a gift, and be grateful for what it brings to you. You'd have to look at how it, in some way, helped you, right? Wow, that's a concept, and a game changer, for sure.

Maybe I'm asking you to do something I didn't do all the time myself when I was there. On the other hand, maybe I was more grateful than anyone could know. The point is that NOW is your chance in this life to open up to gratitude for it all. You've got so much assistance from this side to help you understand things. If only you truly knew that all you have to do is ask, and be clear enough to listen—then you'd see your answers. We're all just waiting to hear from you. Please, RSVP!

Oh, and that country thing—there really is enough for everybody there on earth, I mean everybody.

The last trip Vicki took before leaving the Peace Corps was, oddly enough, to the very first 'exotic' destination Jim and I went in the early years of our marriage: the Canary Islands, located off the coast of northern Africa, south of Spain. At that time, the country was just beginning to entertain the tourist trade. We envisioned that there would be yellow birds flying, singing sweetly in a lush, green tropical setting. Instead, on the ride from the airport to the hotel, we were greeted by blowing trash, nobody speaking a word of English, and lots of volcanic rock! A lot has changed in the meantime; it has since become a favorite vacation destination for many, offering to its visitors everything from riding camels, climbing a volcano, romping on the beach, to skydiving. Vicki wanted to escape the cold of the winter in Moldova, and she researched a way to get to the islands on a shoestring budget. That's how people must live in the Peace Corps, and she didn't have trouble with doing that. I remember her emails to us, sharing moments of her solo adventure as she explored the island and watched the sun set over the waters, a welcome experience after being landlocked for a couple of years. We were so happy for her.

Hey, all I wanted out of being there, in that world, was the joy of the experience. You know, maybe that's why you went there, too. The answer to happiness: living in the world, knowing you are not of it—finding joy in the NOW that Is!

The summer after Vicki returned from the Peace Corps, Daniel was adjusting to life outside his service in the military, and we were all living together in our family home. We could each sense Vicki's discomfort; her negativity was silently screaming out at us, and we were saddened by it. My heart felt her pain, and it seemed that the only thing I could do was remind her as often as I could that I loved her. At the time, I wondered if my words made a difference, but I am so grateful that I spoke them, especially then, even if she didn't hear what I was saying. It wasn't easy for any of us to see her hurt and not be able to help her. It was clear that she didn't want help. As in the past, she was continuing to make her own choices coping with her life.

Hey, I heard it all! Humans record every single word they hear, every experience they have—everything. It's all stored inside that mind, downloaded just like you download something on a computer. It's so much better to have 'good' stuff to work with. Earthlings have taken the game of creating a little too far. Those thoughts all of you have had from the beginning of time, both positive and negative, are still floating around there, and that mind of yours latches on to everything, and can mix you all up. I thought I was going out of mine! You know, now is an excellent time for the game to move to a higher place, for everybody's sake. All those thoughts coming into me from all over the place, it was pretty hard to live with. I mean, it took a lot out of me, and it pulled me in many directions. I didn't understand it then. It was not until I left that I finally understood where I had been. But, I do now, and maybe everything was right on schedule for me . . . .

Vicki's last job was that of an insurance fraud investigator. I guess that's what you could call it. She did surveillance work observing people who were thought to be collecting disability money fraudulently. She sat, incognito, in a little white van glued to a camera for the entire day, watching people, watching every little move—recording them, perched and ready to jump into the driver's seat and race behind them through crowded city streets to unknown destinations. She was unable to move for hours at a time. She learned quickly that if she took her eyes off the camera, she could lose her suspect and waste an entire day's work. Vicki always did her job to the best of her ability, and she did a fine one for this company, earning a special notice of appreciation for her surveillance efforts soon after her first months at work. We had concern for her; the hours and conditions were horrendous. She got up sometimes in the middle of the night to drive hours to her destination, arriving before the sun was up so she could track a suspect's every move before the day began. It was part of her work ethic. She valued the quality of the job she did, no matter what it was. Sometimes she was away for a few days on a case, staying overnight in a motel. She always managed to find an inexpensive one in which to stay, sacrificing her own comforts for the company. In the winter months in the northeast, it was so cold sitting in the van, immobile, staring at a camera monitor for hours on end. She had a little heater, but that didn't help much. She had to bundle up, and her feet would freeze, but she was used to freezing temps in Moldova. Still, it wasn't comfortable, that's for sure. She had to monitor any bathroom breaks because she could lose her subject in an instant, so she would have to 'go' inside the van in the cold. We bought her a portable potty that she never used. She could brave tough circumstances without complaint. Vicki always did what she thought she had to do. If a subject left their home, she had to track them, and sometimes she would have to speed carefully through the streets to keep up, always with her eyes riveted on the person she was following. Sometimes she would end up lost, herself, in a city or a section she knew nothing about and would have to find her own way back home.

I remember her describing one particularly scary moment. She was parked out on a lonely country road inside her van whose windows were coated in black, and heavily curtained. The subject lived up on a hill, and she could not easily hide, so she was forced to station her van at the base of the hill in order to observe if and when he left his home. It was all pretty obvious, and the subject easily caught on to the strategy. He charged down the hill and angrily approached the little van parked out in the middle of nowhere. Vicki was behind the darkened windows, and the man proceeded to beat on them in a rage, shouting obscenities and threats at her. It must have been terrifying. She shared with me what an upsetting moment it was for her, but what bothered her more is that she hated poking her nose into other people's business—analyzing and judging their every move. That's what troubled her the most.

The symbolism of me in that little van, unable to move, spying on people, just watching their every move, in the dark ... man, isn't that the bottom of the barrel? Sort of described where I was at that time, didn't it? Exposed on the landscape of life, hiding in a shell, the world attacking me, spewing all its negativity right at me, until I had had enough. No wonder I left. Perhaps my being there was complete. Perhaps I had learned enough.

It used to bother me there to see people not caring about connecting. You know people who don't even notice you, don't smile, just ignore you. The easiest way to notice is to use your smile. It's a reminder to someone and yourself that we're all connected. It's like a little secret shared—a vibrational shot in the arm. But again, everybody has their reasons for what they are choosing to do. Everybody has a different perspective, but man, life there would be a lot nicer if you'd just wake up and see some things! Humanity could use an attitude adjustment. The sooner you each know that the energy you are comes from the same

Source, that you are unique extensions of The All, maybe you could truly feel appreciation, compassion and connection. Life there would change, that's for sure. Maybe that's what the game's all about.

On the way to a surveillance job one icy late winter morning, just a month before she made the decision to leave this Earth, Vicki was in an accident, and the company van was totaled. Despite the setback, a replacement van was immediately arranged, and Vicki went out on a job. But later, while carrying heavy equipment, she slipped on the ice and subsequently broke a bone in her ankle, which then put her on leave for a month. She was quite shaken over the accident, more than we knew. She had been so fearless for so long, and we were a bit surprised at her reaction. I guess only she knew how close to leaving this life she had come that day. Vicki just knew things that she didn't always let us know, and looking back on it, maybe she had some deeper knowledge that she was getting close to changing her 'location' so to speak. It seemed that Vicki traveled to other places—other realities—easily, and what happened for her in those places, I do not know.

Yep, I knew my time was coming close, I'd gone my distance. You see, we all have opportunities to leave or stay many times in a life there. Remember those times when you could have easily left that world? I mean accidents, times when you said, "OMG, that was close!" Well, here's the news: it really is your choice when and how it's going to happen. Okay, maybe you don't consciously know that at the time, but that doesn't rule it out as a possibility. After all, wouldn't it be a more interesting and challenging game not to know these things? The point is, when anyone leaves, no matter how, why do people then have to judge it? Spirit energy leaves when it decides to go, and that's its business. It has its own reasons, no matter how it left. Something deeper is going on with all of you—all of us. How something happens doesn't matter for the one who left. When all the 'dust' settles, LOL, the real question is for the ones who are left behind, still in the game. What will they choose as a result? How will they use this change to grow in the game of life?

In the quiet days following the car accident, while she recovered from the ankle injury, Vicki had the opportunity to think about her future. She finally decided to complete that application to graduate school, the one she had been toying with for a long time—the one that would begin her journey toward earning a master's degree in psychology. She wisely used her time off by completing and then sending the application before the deadline. She had a sense of satisfaction about it, and so did I. All she needed to do was wait to hear the results. We had talked numerous times throughout the years about how intelligent I knew she was, and we both saw her going to school and earning further degrees. While she filled out her application, we were on the phone together verifying information. I had the privilege of editing her final essays. It was a joy to read her thoughts on paper. I was so encouraged by her responses that I took the liberty to share them with her father, sister and brother, unbeknownst to her. I did it because Vicki still managed to maintain a separateness about herself, and we never knew quite what was going on with her. After reading her essays, we all felt a sense of direction now coming from her, like she was on some solid ground in her life. Something quite interesting to me now are these words from her rough-draft notes: *It seems in my life whether I planned it or not, I have found myself in positions of observing people and human behavior ... My interest in communicating with those I may observe is heightened from living in an environment where I could observe but not communicate (Moldova) ... With my current job I observe people without them knowing ... it can be very interesting at times . . . .*

My last conversation with Vicki while she was in her earthly body was shortly before she was to, once again, leave on a job after the time she had taken off due to the broken ankle bone. She busily readied herself for the trip that was to happen in a couple of days. She needed to send some equipment through the mail back to company headquarters, and she was frustrated at the delays that were taking place in the packing and shipping of everything. There were all kinds of miscommunications with telephone operators and people giving out incorrect information. She was upset with the entire situation and tried to explain to me just how disturbing and pointless this waste of time and energy was to her. She just couldn't understand why it had to be this way. She knew that she was being curt with people, and it felt to me as though that really bothered her.

I hated getting mad at people—giving in to a lower vibration. That's weird to say—hated and mad—two wrong way trains going in the same direction ... hmm. Anyway, I was getting tired of feeling that. But because of my experience there, I can see both sides of this. Perhaps people who get angry there aren't really angry at you, they're angry at themselves for other reasons. If you would look at it that way, you'd be more understanding of them. I could have done that more there. I guess all the negative energy was finally getting to me. No matter how people act toward you there, they have their reasons, and most of the time they don't even know why themselves. It can take a lifetime or more to work that out. So, it's patience—patience with yourselves and with others. I know I could have been more patient. I tried, but I went about as far as I could go. Maybe I just knew it was time. Maybe I knew I could do more for the world from this side. Maybe. Time will tell—there's that time thing again!

It was three days after Vicki's and my birthdays and on Jim's birthday that I received the phone call that would change all our lives. Elizabeth and Daniel were living in New York City and Vicki was using our family home in Pennsylvania while she worked her insurance surveillance jobs. I had just returned from Palm Sunday church service in North Carolina when Jim, who was in Utah at the time, delivered the devastating news to me. Vicki had shot herself; she had made the decision to end this Earthly life by her own hand. My heart stood still, and all I could do was sink to the floor screaming, "No!"

We were all stunned and filled with grief as any family would be at the loss of a loved one in any circumstance. I can say that for Jim and me there was something oddly familiar about it because it felt like something sadly and strangely was fulfilling itself. My husband's first words to me over the telephone that day were, "She did it!" I don't know if he even realized he said them. It was as if somehow we knew on some level this was going to happen. It was some time after the initial shock that we became aware of that possibility.

I was pretty disappointed in people, the way they are there, and before I knew it, I got—I guess you could say—disoriented. I knew I wasn't doing what I set out to do. My train was going in the wrong direction and no longer reflected my highest and best. Hey, things can get way out of whack there. Okay, it's like this: if there are kids playing a game of some sort, let's say, baseball—my favorite Earth sport—and they start to forget that it's a game and they run all over the place on the field—go nuts, well, the umpire, or whoever is in charge, has to calm them down, start the game all over again. I did that for myself, I called time out so I could regroup and change up my 'game'. In other words, like you've likely heard from another well-known source of wisdom, I had to 'die' to my 'old self' and be 'resurrected' to new life! The thing is, I didn't have to choose to literally do it that way there. I could have chosen to stay and slug it out, but I didn't. I picked my own way to deal with my circumstances. Not to worry. If I hadn't made my life so big in the plus and minus departments, you wouldn't be reading this now. I guess I pushed the envelope, once again. Hey, what did you expect from me? ☺

Victoria Louise Van Meter

Birth on Earth Day: 3/13/82

Transformation Day: 3/16/08

Endings & Beginnings

We're all on our own timeline.

When the time is right for you to 'get something' you do,

and that's how it is.

They remembered all the happiness the little lantern had
    brought,
The gift of warmth that was the light and the battles it
    had fought.
Why did the little lantern suddenly leave ... why did it
    move along?
And they searched inside themselves to see where they
    went wrong.

Perhaps, the little lantern's message is one for me and you
We need to watch what it is we think, say, and do.
For when we spout out soot in our thoughts, and words,
    and deeds,
We dim the lights around us when *more light* is what we
    all need.

I think I'll shake this family up . . .
I think I'll rock the world . . .
Somehow, I'll make it happen!
Bang!
And so it is . . .

Something had happened in my life that I never dreamed would take place; I stood along with my husband, Jim, my eldest daughter, Elizabeth, and my son, Daniel, in a back room of a funeral home, stunned to see my youngest child's still body lying on a cold, steel table. The room was filled with cries of pain, disbelief, tears, but something unexpectedly beautiful happened in this experience, as well. The room filled with the warm glow of this child's spirit. A radiance beamed from her perfect, peaceful form and the grace and wisdom of her true being surrounded us. We asked for her help in getting us through the rest of our lives, lives that we knew had to be lived without her. She definitely heard our pleas, for her continued presence with us from that moment forward to this day is unmistakable.

You know, the coolest thing was that you were all open enough to receive the real me at that moment! It was as special for me knowing that you felt me there. I mean, it can be rather confusing for a while as you are transitioning to this side, but you guys really caught on quickly. I know, you didn't think you did because you were still shocked and sad, but you did—especially you, Mother, and that made everything so much easier for me!

Now, some thoughts on transitioning—that's what it is—nothing dies, it just changes form. Hey, you can't destroy energy, can you? I hope you know by now that the body, although an important vehicle for you while you are on earth, disappears, blends itself back into the soil from which it was born. By the way, you should spend some time taking care of that machine you're wearing for the time you have it to use. Did I say that before? Well, I'm just sayin' it again!

So, all creation came from a big bang! The thought of the Creator sent love to live in all parts of everything. Our Birth on Earth came from a big bang of love between two people, and my birth into where I live now was another big bang for me, and I was here! I was birthed into another place, or dimension, if you will, and I can tell you that this birth, too, came from a place of love. You don't have to understand that, but I do now, and eventually you might, too, in your own time. I guess I can say that sometimes, you just know when you're supposed to leave a place and go somewhere else; you just know. Maybe I was remembering it was my plan all along to gather as much of the negative as I could, and take it out of the world so there would be less for you all to deal with. Now that's rockin', isn't it?

Wow, the relief for me! I was under so much pressure with all that distraction surrounding me. It's there, believe me: false beliefs, negative thought forms, greed, jealousy, anger, pain—the list goes on and on. I mean I tried to adjust, but ... something told me I needed the break, a vacation of sorts. The best way to explain what living there was like for me is this: I was walking in a big pool of water up to my neck; my head was above the water, in the real world, the one you can't see, and the rest of my body was submerged under the water in that world that you think is 'real', but actually isn't. Trying to walk, to move forward under all the pressure that surrounded me was getting too difficult. I felt crushed, and I couldn't breathe. You know how hard it is when you are trying to walk in a swimming pool, how slow it feels? Everything took so long, and I could feel all that distraction deep inside. But I wasn't desperate; I wasn't fearful of being in the pool. Swimming is fun, isn't it? I just knew that I could pop myself out of the water to go back from where I had come, and something inside of me went for it. Maybe I made my choice on purpose because I wanted it that way.

This is just my story. Although we are all connected, we each have our own story. We deal with the same kinds of issues, they just look different on the outside to other people. You have to make your own choices in your life there. From where I am now, looking back on things, I see what an awesome opportunity a life there is, and you need to know that. It's a real gift for the chance to feel all kinds of things through experiences and all the emotions they bring. Hey, like I said, you are love; you came from it, and you return to it, and that's cool. But to have the chance to feel something else and to actually be able to physically touch things that are in material form? Well, as you'd say there, that's priceless! So, be happy to feel something, whatever it is!

Some people might say I left because of my experience of flying at an early age. Well, is it so hard to see that maybe I was meant to fly when I came there to show people, kids, girls, what they can do? It would have been nice not to have to live in sooty thoughts and all, but it's the risk we all take when we come there, and it's worth it to experience everything. It all works out ... eventually. It just takes time to see it all, and maybe a change of scenery, if you know what I mean. ☺

Don't be so hard on those people who leave by choice. Maybe they had a reason, a good one that you aren't supposed to know about right now. I know when my dad was meditating one day and started to ask me why I left like I did, I stopped him before he even got the question out and told him not to give it a second thought—it was just the fastest way to get here. I also told him that the kind of help I needed I couldn't get there—I had to be here, and now I am getting all the help I need. That's the truth for me. You have your reasons for every important thing you do, right? Sometimes you don't even know why you do something, you just listen to your gut and you act. When you hear your heart speaking, that's even bigger. I heard one of my friends there tell my mother that if people try to understand with their heads why I left, they'd never get it, but if they go through their hearts and touch the soul, they will. She said that I lived from my soul, and looking back on it, you can say that. Another thing—is it so far-fetched to think that all people in some way create the 'when' and 'how' they will shed their vehicle and leave the earth? I know the answer to that. ☺

I left a note that said, "Take comfort in knowing there was nothing anyone could have said or done to prevent this from happening." That's the truth, so please take comfort and lay off the judging of yourselves, will you? Maybe you are supposed to learn something from your 'loss' no matter what the circumstance. There is a divine plan and we are all part of it, each and every one of us. Everyone and everything is woven together in that gorgeous tapestry connected by unseen threads! I know it sounds sort of crazy when you're there, but it's true. It is your choice to trust in the mystery of it all, or not. If you do, your NOW will be much easier to BE in. I'm just sayin'. ☺

Although the words of Vicki's note did bring us some comfort, it was still a struggle to reach a point of some kind of understanding. Understanding grows with time. We all had adjustments to make in our lives after Vicki's decision to leave this plane, but as difficult as it was for us, Elizabeth, Daniel, and I knew it was the most challenging for Jim. We were all aware of a special connection he had with her. In some respects the two were very much alike, and Jim enjoyed that bond with her when she was little, but as she grew into maturity, there were some rocky times when their relationship changed. I used to encourage his patience with her, and it was hard for a while, but fortunately they grew closer in the last years of her time here. And shortly after she left, Vicki began coming to Jim in his dreams. It seemed that when he had a question in his mind, she would come to him while he slept, to answer it.

I think Jim would admit that he has looked back at how he could have been different in the years gone by in a way that would have been easier for Vicki and everyone in the family, and he has regrets. That's only normal. He struggled to forgive himself. In one of his dreams he conveyed to her that he would handle it all so differently now, with more understanding. In response, she spoke, *"I would, too, Dad. I can see things in a whole new way now, too."*

I sure can. Hey, Dad, forget it! Forgiveness is a circle that comes back to you. It starts with forgiving yourself, and when you do that, something really cool happens: your heart opens up, and then you can let it flow to the other guys—the other parts of you—because whether you want to believe it or not, everyone and everything is part of you. And actually, there isn't anything to forgive if judgment is out of the picture, is there? That judgment thing, it turns around and bites you in the butt real quick, doesn't it? But, as long as you're doing it there, you've got to use that forgiveness release button, and start with yourself, please. I ended up getting trapped on that one. Don't get me wrong, I'm not judging myself now; I'm not in a place that does that. I'm just saying some things that might help you while you are there having an experience. The sooner you get that everything there just is, I mean really get it, the struggle's over and the fun stuff comes, and who doesn't want the fun stuff? I know that part was the best for me. Oops, that's a judgment!

And while I'm on the subject of forgiveness, I've got something else to say. Forgiving can actually be very easy to do because when you think about it, it's a selfish act and you people there think a lot about yourselves, but sometimes you do it for the wrong reasons. When you hold resentment and junk inside, you clog up the place where the real you lives, and you can't hear any of the good stuff, or at least it's much harder to hear it. All of that negativity turns into soot inside of you and when you talk or act, it can come shooting out into the atmosphere, polluting everything! You should all be concerned about that kind of pollution.

Anyway, what someone said to you or did to you is in the past. Said, did, the minute it's out, it's in the past. This is NOW! How much easier to let it go the sooner it comes out, and believe me, breathing there will be much better. Haven't you had lots of very wise, ground-breaking people tell you that all through the ages? Your 'sins' are forgiven ... they are, people!

Look at it closer. We all choose to experience all kinds of things. The word out there from God is quite emphatic. There is no sin; all is forgiven. Didn't someone come there and go through a lot of 'pain' and 'suffering' to show you that? That doesn't mean you go around doing those bullying things to everybody because you know you'll be forgiven! It means when you are clear inside, you listen to the things that are helpful to say and do to your fellow man and to all living creatures, including yourself! That's a personal responsibility. It's all a circle of love. Forgiveness is part of it. And so is gratitude.

The big one to forgive is yourself because you are part of that mix. Just change the way you think about it, and you will be forgiving people all over the place, from the past, to the now, and believe it or not, you'll be ready and willing to forgive what will happen. You'll be making more room inside for lots of good things, and life will get so much easier. Eventually, when you're in this space, where I am now, everything is wiped out anyway, so why not get a head start on feeling good while you are there? Let me tell you, the bliss here is pretty indescribable! I wish I'd have forgiven sooner there. Maybe I had inside, but I could have chosen to show it more. You all know this is true; you feel better when you do forgive, don't you? It's like something inside is cleared and you smile more. Hey, I'm just sayin' . ☺

It was Thanksgiving the year after Vicki left, and Jim and I were celebrating without Elizabeth and Daniel, who were both unable to get home to be with us. I was in the kitchen preparing a traditional turkey dinner along with all the trimmings for Jim when he took a break from working inside our attached garage to follow the smells of freshly baked pie and savory turkey luring him back inside.

As I peeled potatoes at the sink, Jim raised his hands in prayer to our 'unseen' daughter: "Vicki, can you please be here with us today?" I quickly reassured him that she already was, and he acknowledged it, but still, he was asking for the impossible: for her return.

Jim solemnly made his way back to the garage to continue working, and perhaps to contemplate his feelings on this family day of giving thanks. I was at the computer checking out a recipe when I got a phone call from Jim, urgently, yet calmly, asking me to come out to the garage. With so much yet to do on the dinner, even though his tone was a curious one, I exasperatedly marched out the door of the house into the garage, then turned to my right, the car directly behind me. I faced Jim with the question, "Okay, what do you want?" He asked me to turn around slowly, and when I did, I understood everything. Not two feet from me, resting on the hood of our car was a beautiful white and gray bird. It had flown in through the open garage door, landing right next to Jim as he worked there.

We were astounded, because the bird did not leave. Following my motherly instincts, I went inside, filled one bowl with water and another with some food from our community bird seed stash which we shared with all our bird visitors in our backyard. I hurried to the garage to find the bird still there, and when I gently placed my gift on the car hood, the bird stepped forward and began eating and drinking. We didn't quite know what to do. We were in awe that the bird was still there as the sun was starting its descent.

Leaving the garage door open so the bird could have its freedom to leave, we went inside to eat our meal. When we checked back later that night, the bird was no longer on the hood, so we closed the garage door, feeling the special blessing this unexpected visitor brought to us on Thanksgiving Day.

In the garage the next morning, as we re-examined the scene of the previous day, we became puzzled as we noticed bird feed on the floor. My gaze moved upward to the top of an inside door to an adjoining storage room, and caught the most amazing sight; the bird had never left; it was roosting on the open door above us. Remarkable!

But the most remarkable thing is that our *Little Buddy* stayed with us for two months. Jim built a small hutch inside the little storage area for her to use as a home base. We fed her regularly, supplying all her needs, and we opened the garage door periodically to let her fly in the neighborhood. I watched her silvery-white wings flapping in the cobalt blue sky as she went on practice flights around a racetrack in the sky above our home. *Little Buddy* would land on a rooftop peak across the street and observe us, but as the day ended, she would find her way back to her home inside our garage.

When Jim worked in the garage, *Little Buddy* followed him around the shop, hiding, hardly visible among the myriad antique signs and fixtures Jim had hung on the walls above him. In the days before *Little Buddy* left us, she started to coo to Jim as he worked in the garage. I could hear the sweet sound through the door: Jim's secret message from our little friend.

On the day *Little Buddy* chose to leave, a storm was brewing, and we were surprised that she had not returned to the security of her home in our garage by day's end. Jim's reaction was not one of pain and sadness, but instead, one of hope and faith that she had arrived safely at another important destination. *Little Buddy*, the carrier pigeon, who answered Jim's plea to Vicki on that Thanksgiving Day, brought him peace.

You've got messages all around you, people—all of you—just pay attention and believe what you are seeing and feeling. Look, we are leaving all kinds of messages for you, all the time. You just have to open your heart up to knowing they are real! I know, it can be amazing to you what we can orchestrate from over here, but it is completely natural to us!

Vicki's voice spoke to me, too, as I slept in those first days, gently telling me, "No more tears, Mother." I knew it was she, because it sounded just like something she would say to me. I found myself listening and having more strength in the days, months and years ahead, more than I ever knew I had. I know I have had help from Vicki. It was her gift to me; the one that keeps on giving.

When I was a little girl, for a short time my mother tried to earn some extra money for our family by selling cosmetics. Perhaps I am assuming that it was for that reason. I suppose it was possible that as a stay-at-home mom, which was typical for mothers at that time, she was pursuing a need to express herself in a different way. Regardless, I remember quite clearly her glamorous white embossed cosmetic case that held treasures beyond my imagination.

I was thrilled as she practiced her sales demonstration for me, revealing the mysteries of grown-up beauty! She removed each of the tiny tubes that lined the bottom row inside the box, allowing me to experience the loveliness of the brightly colored lipstick each one held. Oh, the excitement of it all! Then, she moved on to the row of mini-vials of liquids filled with entrancing essences and perfumes.

Mother held a special one forward for me and said, "This is very truly yours," and as I reached out my little hand and took the precious gift, I was filled with such joy in knowing that it was mine to keep. It was given by my mother to me—my own personal treasure. But soon after, she took it from my adoring hand, and I realized that it was not mine at all. *Very Truly Yours* was just the name of the perfume.

My happiness of the moment disappeared and reality set in, but now, I have this sweet story to tell. My gift had been temporary, but I will always remember the joy that was mine in having received it, no matter how long it stayed nestled within my hands.

Perhaps, this is a parent's message. Our children are gifts from the heavens that we believe belong to us when we receive them. Gifts, yes, but ours they are not. We do not own them. We cannot own them. They belong to themselves. They are creations of God loaned to us for just a moment in the eternity of existence. We are privileged to hold them for only a second in time, and isn't that true of anyone we love? I now know how profound my experience with Vicki was and continues to be. I also know that our family wasn't quite ready for me to share the extent of our story until we all expanded into deeper understanding of ourselves, our relationship to each other, and to her. That has taken years, and it's still happening; it never ends.

Yes, it took a while, but I worked with all of them, until they

saw me there, right alongside them in each of their lives. Hey, I'm still working with them—holding space for them in their play, like I did in that Brownie play when I was little there. Cooperation is a good thing! You should see what's happened to my whole family since I left. But that's another story, a wonderful one.

We are now loaded with a treasure trove of Vicki weaving herself into our lives. Funny, but once you start to notice the messages, they come more often and with much more clarity. That's how it happens. Once, while walking down the hall after a full morning's successful work on a website for Vicki, my cell phone began to play that Irish barroom song we had sung years ago while meandering the roads of Ireland. It was so unexpected that even *Mya* was startled. And speaking of the dogs—there is one particularly priceless story of Vicki showing herself through them.

One of Vicki's favorite things to do on Halloween was to dress her dogs, *Mya* and *Jose*, in silly costumes. She loved to slick back feisty, toothless *Jose's* long, white Maltese hair into a mohawk, spiking it with pink, neon-colored kool-aid. She seemed to take pleasure in the absurdity of it, laughing as she did it. A couple of years after Vicki left, we were finally settled in our new home out west, along with the two dogs. It was Halloween, and Jim and I carried on the tradition, dressing the dogs up and taking them trick-or-treating in our neighborhood. *Mya*, not appreciating the indignity of it all, and obviously feeling encumbered by my choice for her, wore a red and black spotted ladybug costume on her back, and had to be pulled along the sidewalk as we made our rounds. *Jose*, on the other hand, absolutely loved the opportunity to cross-dress into a pink princess outfit made of satin, lace and netting, complete with a cone shaped hat flowing with chiffon, secured with elastic around his head. He loved it, and it showed! We knew Vicki was smiling as he pranced with pride alongside a reluctant bug.

Later, at nighttime, we were in our bed winding down from a full day. Earlier, Jim had put the finishing touches on a treatment I had chosen for the wall above the headboard of our bed. It was fun to choose new and meaningful looks for what we knew would probably be the last home we would have in this life cycle. I had chosen a stencil of a phrase to put there, one that was inspiring to both of us. It read: *Every day holds the possibility of a miracle.* It was perfect. We lay in our bed, in our new home, those words above us, and we were happy to know that we had created a sweet day for Vicki's dogs, one that brought her joy. It had done that for us, as well.

Okay, here's the back story. We never allowed the dogs to sleep in our bed, and so, because Jose had his problems controlling himself around the house, our solution was to keep him on a long leash attached to a large hook on the outside of a cabinet in our tile-floored kitchen. We could keep him off our bed that way, and we would not run into any 'deliberate accidents' all over our house. If *Mya* was not in his presence, our special needs Maltese would bark incessantly, so she sacrificed her freedom and was leashed along *Jose*—separate leashes, but attached to the same large hook. This system had worked for years, even in our family home back east.

So, there we were in our bed, on this special day, feeling content, when we heard a strange noise slowly making its way down the long, tiled hallway toward our bedroom door. Perplexed, we sat up, turned the lights on, and around the corner of the door frame gingerly peeked two renegade dogs dragging their leashes behind them. Somehow, some way, both of them managed to be released from that hook at the same time, allowing them to make their way together to our room. Jim and I looked at one another, both knowing that Vicki wanted them to hop into bed along with us on this sweet day, one that she had enjoyed, too. So from that day forward we lovingly shared sleeping quarters with our two charges, and we wouldn't have it any other way.

That was slick, huh? Love can do miraculous things. Remember, every day really does hold the possibility of a miracle; you just have to notice them!

I was deeply touched by having Jose in my life, the half blind, Maltese dog that Vicki and I found together and 'rescued.' After he passed on it wasn't very long before I yearned to have a little white dog in my life once again. As the years went by, I kept dropping hints that someday 'when I'm a little old lady,' I'd have a cuddly partner back in my life.

When it looked like even Mya seemed to be missing some canine companionship, Jim suggested we look for my little white dog even though I was not yet that little old lady. We soon found ourselves discouraged by the scams that surround purchasing a dog either online or in the newspaper, so instead, we asked for Vicki's help in bringing a dog to us.

One evening Jim spoke to her and invited her to help us find a dog if she wanted that to happen. The very next day I received a telephone call. It was my friend, Kasey, who, along with being an intuitive, is a fabulous hairdresser. She asked me about the dog I wanted, of which I had often spoken. "What kind of dog is it ... a white Maltese? I have a lady in my chair right now who is looking for a home for a white multi-poo for her friend who is very ill and can no longer care for the dog."

And so, Tiffany or "Tiffy" came to us. We know Vicki found her for us. She's just the right match for Vicki's sensibilities: she's loving, a wild card, and she needed some help. She was walking alongside me, following me around soon after she became ours, and

I started singing a song to her. "Mary had a little lamb, little lamb, little lamb. Mary had a little lamb …" Then it dawned on me—she looked exactly like a lamb! I smiled a knowing smile. Vicki had chosen a little white dog for me that resembled my favorite animal—a lamb.

While you are living there, you are connected in ways that you'd never believe possible. It's up to you to see what's going on around you and put it together.

The most extraordinary things have happened to us in our home since Vicki left this earth, and we are sure she has had a hand in them. And speaking of incredible events—here's one involving Mya and Tiffany, our dogs, and Barbara, a friend who came to stay at our home to take care of them for a number of weeks while we were gone. Barbara had been watching the dogs for days, taking them for long walks, feeding them special foods, giving them extra treats and loving them in our absence. One day, she was sitting at the kitchen counter perched on a stool, working on her computer when she thought to herself, "I could use something cold to drink." She got up and went to the other end of the house and was diverted for a bit by a chore. When she returned to her place in the kitchen, there, sitting right next to the computer was an open bottle of raspberry green tea. And it was cold! She was amazed—after all, she was the only other person in the house!

After she collected herself, Barbara called us and asked if we had a bottle of raspberry green tea in the refrigerator, as she hadn't even seen one in her days there. Jim told her that there was one odd bottle that had been floating around in the fridge for some time, and it was somewhere way in the back. The only thing left to think was that Vicki was somehow involved. Barbara figured that maybe Vicki listened to her asking for a cold drink, and this was Vicki's way of thanking her for taking care of the dogs. Or, she thought, Vicki might have been letting Barbara know she was hanging around watching her every move with the dogs! Either way, it was astonishing!

What can I say ... it's just freakin' awesome the things we can do! Believe it! And the more you notice, the more we'll do ....

Another incident happened at our friend Tor's house. He created an awesome website about Vicki that includes details about her flights. He made a re-creation of Vicki's trip across the Atlantic which allows the visitor to virtually take the trip along with her, actually landing in each of the airports as she did. I do a voiceover of the journey. We had worked on it for some days, and it was finally completed. We were in awe when we realized that Vicki, a girl of 12, had actually taken this trip in a little single-engine airplane. I remember us following along on the entire trip and just sitting there at the end, almost not being able to take it in. It was then that something equally awesome happened. My cell phone, which was sitting on a table close by, *on its own* started to play a saved message. Tor asked me what it was. I knew immediately. Years before that day, Vicki had left that very message for me on my birthday, which was also hers. I had kept and still have the message on my cell phone. It is so precious to me. She happily surprises me singing, "Happy Birthday, Happy Birthday, Mom, where are you?" As Tor and I sat in amazement of Vicki flying across the Atlantic, she amazed us once again, this time, by visiting us over the telephone wires. I guess she liked the website . . . .

I did ... I really did! ☺

Remember when Vicki was little and she had the code name Dave for getting into the men's restroom? Okay, now for the follow-up to that story: Vicki continues to show up in the most unusual circumstances and most interesting ways. Recently, I had the occasion to be in an elementary school talking to a principal, something not ordinary for me, as I have been retired from teaching for a number of years. I was at the school to find illustrators for another book I had written about Vicki, called *The Little Girl Who Wanted to Fly*. I thought perhaps it would be appropriate that children illustrate Vicki's story, so I chose a school nearby and found myself in the principal's office enthusiastically sharing the story of my daughter's accomplishments, in hopes that she might connect with my project.

I was in the middle of my presentation when it was interrupted by the ring of the principal's cell phone. Not recognizing the number, she answered it anyway. After a very brief exchange, she disconnected and apologized for the interruption, then shared, "It was a wrong number," and then quizzically added, "It was somebody named Dave?" I just smiled and chuckled to myself.

Miracles R Us! ☺

I remember when we were in Ireland on that trip to visit Elizabeth, we wandered into a quaint shop in the Irish countryside and made a small purchase. I was drawn to a collection of little stones which held meaningful scripted sayings upon their backs. One in particular captured my attention. I do not know the fate of that little rock, but I do remember the saying:

> "What we call the beginning is often the end.
> To make an end is to make a beginning.
> The end is where we start from."
> T.S. Eliot

All of us have started over in the never-ending circle of life, including Vicki.

You think I don't remember that rock in Ireland, too? Maybe it looked like I wasn't paying attention. Well, surprise! Interesting that you should choose that rock with that saying, then, and remember it now, isn't it? Mother, you don't need that rock; you know the truth of what's on it. It's written in your heart.

Finally, I see that through this book, which you are reading at this very moment, Vicki is completing the work she had aimed to do here on the earth: flying around the world for kids and helping young people connect more with themselves, as well as with other people. She's just doing it from the other side—combining flying with a different kind of psychology.

I always envisioned her achieving that advanced degree. Maybe she had one all along. I have come to know that perhaps it wasn't that Vicki wasn't ready for the world, but that the world wasn't quite ready for her.

Mother, you've really caught on. ☺

I've thought a lot about Vicki's smile and of her laughter. The light that beamed from her eyes when she was just a child was pure essence from the Soul Source. Even as she grew, and smiles became fewer, the joy of life still poured from her being through her laughter.

Of course, I miss being near the person that was Vicki—that's a human response. But to be in the space where love has been does not have to be a sadness, for love lives within remembrance of itself. When I smile in remembering her, I can still see her smile, and when I laugh as I think of her, I can still feel her joy; they are reminders to me of how very special it is to live in this earth space, in this time. I treasure being able to hear her speak through my words. Just the thought of them helping you in any way, well, it warms my heart, and she's there, too. I live in gratitude for knowing it.

The final verse to that poem is this:

So when you see a lantern shining brighter than the rest
Please give that lantern your highest love … give all lanterns and
    yourself your very best
So you may see light's beauty in your day and in your night,
And in your heart will shine the *wisdom of the light!*

My Recap: I've shared a lot about my life there in the world, but you won't know everything 'cause, frankly speaking, some things are meant to be only known by just us, right? Hey, my mother doesn't know everything I've done. She's pretty sure she has some idea, but not everything! Right … well, I've got news for you … it's all pretty much an open book from up here. To us, it's like we're watching a game being played, or a play going on, and there isn't any judging about winning or losing anything. Hey, it's all meant to be enjoyed by the players. All of it. Yes, even the struggles. There's a lot of experiencing going on! It's only painful if you want it to be. I did experience pain there. Now I see that it was my choice to do that, but if I didn't allow that to happen, I wouldn't be sharing this awesome information with you now.

If everything had gone just cool for me in my life after the flying thing, you probably wouldn't even know I existed, and I'd still be there, maybe playing along with you all in the game. Instead, I'm working it from my side to let you know what's going on, to help you enjoy the game while you are there, if you want the help, that is. The truth of the matter is, you already know all this stuff I've been saying to you; you just have to remember it!

I remember an interview I gave when I was flying. The

interviewer asked me how it felt to be a role model. I never looked at myself that way, but I do remember telling her that if people thought so, then maybe I could say some things that might help kids. Well, you're all kids—everyone there! Considering that time is never-ending, that means you are growing, always growing, changing shape from moment to moment. Learning never ends. I used to say then that it's all about what you think and how you feel, that if you put your mind to it, you can accomplish anything.

Maybe part of my life there was about showing that to the world, but only I can truly know the meaning of the rest of why I was there. And that's okay. Just take what you choose from my life and learn what you can while you are there.

One last piece of advice: Relax. Life just IS, so enjoy it, every last bite because ALL IS WELL!

I have another verse to add to that poem:

So shine your light, give all you've got ... show who you are,
  hesitate not!
Your light is meant to brightly shine, for who you are is a gift
  divine!
And if by chance, some soot should land upon your shoulder, just
  take your hand
And brush it to the skies above ... I'll return it to you as light and
  love
                              Vicki

That's my story, that's my life the last time around, while I was there, where you are now, and the point is—it happened—all of it! All things considered, it turned out to be a pretty exciting and interesting go-around for me. And my story isn't over yet, I tell you, because I'm still here … do you hear me?

The Little Lantern
...inspired by Elizabeth Forrest & Uncle Will

There was a little lantern lit by the sun,
Its brilliance shone far and wide, but its work wasn't done.
This special little lantern made a journey to earth
And shined its light so very bright from the moment of its birth.

It came with a message from its Creator above.
It was filled with all possibility wrapped in a blanket of love.
Light disguised in a little lantern, now, who would have thought...
Oh, the importance of that message, the one the little lantern
    brought.

The little lantern listened to direction from back home
And brightly beamed its pure white light; over the world it roamed.
People gathered 'round to see what it could do,
To watch in awe and wonder, and feel inspiration, too.

The little lantern was able to do amazing things.
It bathed the dark in its loving light, transforming everything!
The little lantern held a secret that it hoped the people would know
    was true,
That everyone could use that light, for it was inside of them, too.

The little lantern watched the people dance and smile and play,
And longed to laugh along with them and have a 'normal' day.
So it tried to dim its light so all the people could see
That the lantern was just the same as them ... filled with all
    possibility!

At first it was a little game the lantern thought it could play,
But transforming darkness into light became tougher each day.
The little lantern was weakening and it began to fear
That it would not be long before all its light would disappear.

Then something troubling happened outside the lantern, it's true,
It grew clouded with sadness; only a tiny light could shine through.
People's cruelty and judgment, their jealousy and fear
Had soiled the glass on the lantern, its light could no longer appear.

And so the little light hid from everyone,
And soon it knew its journey here was finished, it was done.
And when it left to shine again in places unknown,
Earth's people talked of how much more brightly it could have shown.

They remembered all the happiness the little lantern had brought,
The gift of warmth that was the light and the battles it had fought.
Why did the little lantern suddenly leave ... why did it move along?
And they searched inside themselves to see where they went wrong.

Perhaps, the little lantern's message is one for me and you ...
We need to watch what it is we think, say, and do.
For when we spout out soot in our thoughts, and words, and deeds,
We dim the lights around us when more light is what we all need.

So when you see a lantern shining brighter than the rest,
Please give that lantern your highest love ... give all lanterns and yourself your very best
So you may see light's beauty in your day and in your night,
And in your heart will shine the wisdom of the light!

So shine your light, give all you've got ... show who you are, hesitate not!
Your light is meant to brightly shine for who you are is a gift divine!
And if by chance, some soot should land upon your shoulders, just take your hand
And brush it to the skies above ... I'll return it to you as light and love....

Corinne and **Vicki** Van Meter

Taken inside a kiva at Mesa Verde in Colorado, 7 months after Vicki left.

Notice the spirit light guiding Corinne up the ladder? I told you ... *I'm still here!*

Corinne Van Meter is interested in hearing your stories. To share your experiences with her or for information regarding the possibility of Corinne speaking to your group, please contact her website: www.ananchoroflight.com or write to her at the following address:

Victoria Press
565 Ridgecrest Circle
St. George, UT 84770

To reach Vicki simply close your eyes, think of me and listen. I'll be there ... ☺

www.ingramcontent.com/pod-product-compliance
Lightning Source LLC
LaVergne TN
LVHW051118080426
835510LV00018B/2116